RICH'S

A Southern Institution

JEFF CLEMMONS

THE
History
PRESS

Published by The History Press
Charleston, SC 29403
www.historypress.net

Front cover: Photo by Robert D. Klein, courtesy of the Kenan Research Center at
the Atlanta History Center.
Back cover: Photos courtesy of Thomas Asher (Rich's clock) and Kenneth Rogers, courtesy of
the Kenan Research Center at the Atlanta History Center (Rich's Great Tree).

Unless otherwise noted, all images are from the author's collection.
The ornamental section breaks (glyphs) used in this book reference M. Rich & Bros. Co.'s
early "star and crescent" logo.

First published 2012
Second printing 2012

Manufactured in the United States

ISBN 978.1.60949.191.8

Library of Congress CIP data applied for.

Notice: The information in this book is true and complete to the best of our knowledge. It is
offered without guarantee on the part of the author or The History Press. The author and
The History Press disclaim all liability in connection with the use of this book.

For

Thomas Asher, Norman Asher and Anne Berg,
who opened the doors to Rich's

and

Pat Pepper, Mary Hood and Virginia Spencer Carr, who are my mentors

and

My family and friends, who put up with me during the researching and
writing of this book

CONTENTS

ACKNOWLEDGEMENTS

It is my pleasure to acknowledge the many people who have helped make this book a reality.

First, I want to thank my editors, Jessica Berzon and Will McKay, and The History Press for allowing me the opportunity to write my first book; it has truly been a learning and worthwhile experience.

I am indebted to Thomas Asher and Anne Berg of The Rich Foundation for opening their archives, memories and lives and connecting me to the numerous individuals who ultimately contributed to this book. Additionally, I owe a debt of gratitude to Norman Asher, who also provided me with invaluable connections and assistance in my research efforts. Without this trio, *Rich's: A Southern Institution* would not exist as it does.

I am equally indebted to Kim Blass, Carl Dendy, Nathalie Dupree, Shelia Kamensky Gerstein, Lonnie King, Blondean Orbert-Nelson, Patricia Pflum, Jay Salzman, Jim Seigler and Neil Shorthouse for allowing me to interview them in regards to the numerous events they were involved with, or knew about, at Rich's over the years. In particular, it has been a privilege to converse with Lonnie and Blondean, whose courageous efforts during the Atlanta sit-in movement changed the city and helped get John F. Kennedy into the White House. In regards to Kennedy, I owe author Jack Bass many thanks for his assistance in helping me get the facts surrounding Kennedy's 1960 presidential campaign correct.

Jim Sluzewski and Melissa Goff at Macy's, Inc. have been instrumental in providing me with information about Rich's, Federated Department Stores and Macy's. Their patience to my numerous inquiries is much appreciated. So, too, is the allowance by Macy's to use many of its photographs within my work (Federated Department Stores, Inc.'s corporate name became Macy's, Inc. in 2007).

At Stevens & Wilkinson, Inc., Preston Stevens Jr., Tom Ramsey and Kim Thompkins greatly assisted me in ferreting out the architectural details of all things Rich's. In particular, architect Donald Campbell is to be praised for his help in answering repeated requests from me about particular projects. I thank the firm for allowing me the use of multiple images in my book.

A debt of gratitude goes out to those who were vital confederates to my mission at the following research centers and libraries: the Atlanta History Center's Salvatore "Sal" Cilella Jr., Katherine Hoogerwerf, Betsy Rix, Don Rooney, Melanie Stephan, Deborah Thomas, Sue VerHoef and, in particular, Laura Starratt and Fred Mobley; Emory University Manuscript and Rare Book Library's (MARBL) Elizabeth Chase, Catherine Fernandez and Kathy Shoemaker; Georgia State University Library Special Collections and Archives' Ellen Mary Johnston; and the Georgia Institute of Technology Archives' John Holcombe and Jody A. Thompson.

My neighbor and friend Kerry McCormack deserves special recognition for painstakingly searching microfilm at the Atlanta History Center over several days to find elusive facts. She, as well as Norman Asher, Thomas Asher, Mark Braykovich, Michelle Harlow, Chris Johnson and Hilary Parrish, also read my manuscript with a fine-toothed comb, offering much-needed edits and advice, for which I am greatly appreciative. I am especially grateful for Michelle's time spent with me grammatically ironing out my unconventional writing style.

I offer my appreciation to Sharon Foster Jones, who helped me navigate the world of book writing; to Chad Paulin for his sketch included in this book; to Michael Dabrowa for his assistance with digital preparation of photographic materials; to Dixie Minatra for letting me borrow her trove of Rich's information; to William Hunt, Windsor Herald of Arms, for searching London's College of Arms archives for information regarding Rich's armorial ensigns; to my grandmother, Lois Schairer, who spent many hours searching genealogy websites and ships' logs for information; and to my mother, Joan Schairer, who also assisted with numerous research requests.

A special thank-you also goes out to Irene Kent, who opened her home and reminisced with me about her husband, Sol Kent, and to Morris Rich's great-grandson, Anthony Montag, and his wife, Jackie, who entertained me at their home, where we fondly discussed Rich's and the family that made it great.

Many others also have helped in the development of this book in a multitude of ways, and for their services, advice and favors, I thank Judy Adams, Spring Asher, the Atlanta Preservation Center, Jim Auchmutey, Sandy Berman, William L. Bird, Connie Boyer, Elliott Brack, Virginia Spencer Carr, Aurora Cassirer, CIRCA, Archie Clemmons, Deborah Clemmons, Greg Clemmons, Capri Coffer, Rodney M. Cook Jr., Boyd Coons, Sallie Daniel, Carol Fisk, Jeff Fitz-Randolph, Ellen Fruchtman, Anne Fuentes, Mark Gardner, Ira Genberg, Greg Germani, Matt Gismondi, Martin Goldstein, Carol Tetterton Grantham, Paul Hammock, Ken Hardeman, C. Robert Harrison, Marge Hays, Mary Hood, Barbara Hooten, Elaine Hughes, Patti A. Hughes, John Hutchins, Richard Hyatt, Terry James, Donna Johnson, Sharon Klein, Michael Krauter, Susan Kronick, William B. Laube, Mary-Owen "Morgan" MacDonald, Elizabeth Margo, Judy Marx, Carolyn McLaughlin, Ellen Mendelsohn, Joe Morris, Angela Morris-Long, Angie Bennett Mosier, Sandra Murray, Ellen Nemhauser, Puja Patel, Marcia Gaye Proctor, Dianne Ratowsky, Katie A. Reinsmidt, Robert Reiser, Lyn Nabers Riddle, Rebecca Roberts, Brian P. Roslund, Peter Sachse, Ellen Seigler, Mark Shafer, Sharon Silvermintz, Anita Simon, Randy Stanczyk, Amber L'Amie Stephan, E.J. Stern, Catty Harris Stover, Eileen Stratidakis, Patrice Vance, Elizabeth Vanek, Elaine Walker, Jo Ann Wallace, John Weitnauer and David Whitten.

Finally, I am grateful to my family and friends who have put up with me over the course of this project. I could not have done it without your patience and understanding. Thank you!

To others who helped in the making of this book but have been inadvertently omitted from my acknowledgements, I offer my sincerest apologies.

A Few Words Before

Iknew all about Rich's, or so I thought when I was asked by The History Press to write a book on the company. It was a large department store chain in Atlanta that had been folded into Macy's in the early 2000s, another casualty of a corporate merger. Sure, I had shopped at several Rich's over the years. I knew about the Pink Pig, although I never rode it. I had watched the lighting of The Great Tree on television several times, and at least once in person at Lenox Square, but never at the downtown store atop the Crystal Bridge. And, of course, I had heard people talk about the company's coconut cake as if it was ambrosia made by the gods just for Rich's.

Therefore, when I started to prepare for what you now have in your hands, I thought I would be flushing out the details of what little I already knew and tacking on the largely unrecorded and unknown history of Rich's—those years after 1976 when the chain was no longer family controlled. However, I quickly realized I hardly knew anything about the iconic department store chain, nor, it appeared, did anyone else. Most of the things written on it were incomplete, anecdotal or wholly inaccurate. Thus, I asked The History Press for a deadline extension in order to properly research the firm. I needed more time to document a *true* account of the company, from its horse-and-buggy days to its Internet days. What I uncovered with the extra time was astonishing.

Rich's was fairly well known for its customer service policies, business innovations, community leadership, fashion guidance, goodwill stewardship and, I dare say, for being the communal heart and cultural temple of Atlanta.

But those things, coupled with nostalgic memories of the kiddies' monorail in the shape of a pig, a large Christmas tree and bakery cases full of coconut cakes, are only small parts of a much larger narrative. People have forgotten, or do not know, that Rich's was an astonishingly vast retailing dynasty whose oeuvre spanned from a few years after the American Civil War to the dawning of a new millennium.

At one point in time over its nearly 138-year history, the company consisted of twenty-nine department stores, nineteen stand-alone bakeries, four boutiques, a cooking school, a high school academy, a philanthropic foundation and a discount retailing chain, to name just a few. I have written about these entities herein and the services and events for which Rich's is well known, such as Penelope Penn, Fashionata, The Great Tree and the Pink Pig. I also have examined the people who created Rich's—those who helped build Atlanta architecturally, culturally and spiritually. In fact, most of Rich's history is Atlanta's history; the business was that influential.

Yet a complete and accurate history also includes chapters that people often wish to overlook or ignore. In Rich's case, those might be an early partner's suicide, civil rights protests, the company's acquisition, its parent company's hostile leveraged buyout and bankruptcy woes, the merging of Rich's with Macy's and the eventual removal of the company from the southern retailing landscape. Each of these, however, is an inextricable part of the business's overall story.

My goal upon completing this manuscript was to combine all of Rich's stories together in one place and to provide for the first time a complete, detailed yet unbiased record of the company. I believe I have accomplished that, and I have to admit that I stand in awe of what was once a truly remarkable southern institution.

MIGRATION

HUNGARY FOR AMERICA

Mauritius "Morris" Reich, the founder of what would become Rich's, was born on January 13, 1847, in the centuries-old city of Kaschau, Hungary, modern-day Košice, Slovakia, to Jewish parents Joseph and Rose Reich. He was the fifth of eventually seven children in the Reich household. Morris's parents had spent their whole lives witnessing war. As children, they had grown up through the political fallout of the Napoleonic Wars. Married and with five children, eventually six, they lived through the 1848 Hungarian Revolution and succeeding civil war. By the time Morris was twelve years old, the Reiches had a toddler, their seventh child, and were facing the possibility of their family living through impending war between Sardinia and Austria-Hungary. They feared for their children's futures, whether it was military conscription for their sons or the possibility of all their children living in European-city ghettoes with limited opportunities for a career or owning property, so they set out to get them to America, a country they had heard offered unlimited possibilities for freedom and prosperity.[1]

In 1859, Morris's parents gave him and his older brother, William, sixteen, the majority of their savings and prepared them for their journey abroad. The elder Reiches' plan was to get Morris and William to the Black family in Cleveland, Ohio. Their other children would follow as time and money allowed. The Black family—who had Anglicized their German surname Schwartz, which in Yiddish is shvartz and denotes the color black—had

A mid-1880s formal portrait of Morris Rich. *Courtesy of the Kenan Research Center at the Atlanta History Center.*

known the Reiches in Kaschau but had immigrated to Ohio a few years earlier. Aware of Joseph and Rose's plan to get their children out of Hungary, the Blacks offered to help the boys get set up and established in Cleveland.

With plans in order and finalized, Morris and his brother left Kaschau via stagecoach and traveled to Vienna, Austria. From Vienna, the boys traveled by train to Berlin and then on to Hamburg, Germany. In Hamburg, over the course of a few days, the two arranged passage on a large, wooden steamer ship for a three-week voyage to New York City. The trip at sea would not be an easy, comfortable one for Morris and his brother. They were alone for the first time in their lives, hungry at times, possibly homesick and seasick and traveling in steerage class, cramped with livestock, cargo and other passengers. Additionally, the journey to America was a long one, stretching almost four thousand miles across the North Sea, through the English Channel and over the northern Atlantic Ocean.

When Morris's ship finally did dock in New York Harbor, Lady Liberty was still a little over a quarter of a century away from holding her torch aloft, beckoning immigrants into the country. Morris and his brother, however, were greeted by American immigration services, which asked the two questions about their births, parentage, travels and plans and examined their general health. Once cleared by immigration services, Morris and his brother boarded a train in New York City and headed four hundred miles west to Cleveland, where they would meet the Blacks and start their new, and hopefully better, lives. One of the first steps in creating this new and better life for the brothers was the Anglicization of their surname from Reich to Rich.

Arriving in Cleveland on the southern shores of Lake Erie, Morris and his brother enjoyed a few days of rest and began the process of adjusting to their new homeland. Then, almost immediately, their host family obtained job positions for the two in a local retail store.

After a few weeks of earning pay at his new job, Morris, along with his brother, moved out of the Black household and into a boardinghouse. Morris, armed with little formal education and a bit of watchmaker training he had obtained in Hungary, and his brother, armed with little formal education and a brief apprenticeship as a jeweler in Hungary, were now officially on their own in their newly adopted homeland.

Between 1859, when he first arrived in Cleveland, and 1861, Morris Rich, as he now styled himself, worked as a salesman in various retail outlets in the city. It was also during these first few years in Cleveland that Morris attended night classes and learned to read, write and speak English. Leaving his retail job in 1861, Morris embarked upon a career as a house-to-house salesman. Eventually, this line of work progressed to selling items via horseback in Cleveland and the surrounding area. After a short while, Morris attached a wagon to the back of his horse and entered the more prestigious carriage trade business. Now, Morris could offer his customers a wider array of items to buy, as he did not have to carry only a select few items on his person or strap those items to a single horse.

Morris's brother William during these early years in Ohio eked out his own career selling goods and kept a close eye on his younger brother. Business for both the boys provided enough income to keep them fed, clothed and sheltered. This peaceful, prosperous new existence, however, was not to last. In 1861, the American Civil War broke out and would ravage the boys' newly adopted homeland for four years. Little could they have known that when they left war-torn Hungary, they would so soon be living in the midst of yet another war. Fortunately, however, the brothers avoided military service in the Union army, as they were not U.S. citizens and, therefore, could not be forced to enlist or be pressed into duty. As a result, they continued selling their wares throughout Ohio as war raged across the country.

Undeterred by the outbreak of war in America, Morris's family continued to immigrate into the country. In 1862, Morris's brothers Daniel, eighteen, and Emanuel, thirteen, would join him and William in Cleveland. They, too, would take up selling wares across Cleveland and the Ohio countryside to make a living.

At the end of the American Civil War in 1865, Morris and his three brothers left Ohio and headed south to Georgia. There, the quartet would separate, each settling on different paths in different parts of the region. William would settle in the young town of Atlanta and establish a wholesale business and, later, a whiskey distillery, as well as having business interests in local coal mines. Daniel and Emanuel would peddle goods throughout the state of Georgia before settling down in Albany, Georgia, where they would open a retail enterprise of their own. At the time, they thought Albany offered better business potential than William's chosen city of Atlanta. Morris, meanwhile, would settle just over the Georgia state line in Chattanooga, Tennessee. For a short while, he would work as a retail salesman in the city but would soon give this up and go back to peddling goods via horseback across the state of Georgia, particularly in the north Georgia–Atlanta area.

Over the next decade and a half, Morris's entire family would eventually immigrate to America. His oldest brother, Herman, older and younger sisters Julia and Frances and mother preceded his father in joining the brothers already stateside. Sadly, by the time Morris's father immigrated to America in 1880, his mother had died. She passed away at the age of fifty-eight in 1875, waiting for her husband to join the rest of the family in a migration that had started sixteen years earlier.

SETTLING ON ATLANTA

In 1867, Morris decided to give up the traveling salesman life, plant roots in Atlanta and try his hand at establishing a retail business. His brother William, who had settled in the city at the end of the American Civil War less than two years earlier, had created a successful wholesale business, W.M. Rich & Co., and Morris thought that perhaps he, too, could replicate his brother's success. Additionally, Morris thought the rail system being rebuilt in Atlanta would be perfect for supplying a retail establishment with new goods from across the United States and the world.

Atlanta, like Morris, was just twenty years old. The city had started off as a railroad juncture in 1837 but had two prior names—Terminus and Marthasville—before it was incorporated as Atlanta in 1847. In the aftermath of the American Civil War, the city lay in ruins, was under military rule and was in the first few years of the harsh Reconstruction era, when the

South was being slowly restored to the Union. Yet despite these conditions, people came to the city in droves. The city's population was over twenty thousand in 1867, double what it had been before the war, with many of those pouring back into the city being widows and orphans of Confederate soldiers, citizens who had fled the city when it was under siege in the summer of 1864 or businessmen, such as Morris, looking to get a new start in the devastated South.

What these people found when they returned to Atlanta, however, was a city being haphazardly rebuilt. Hundreds of shanties made from the debris of buildings destroyed in the war stretched across the city. Businessmen also were using this debris to build stores to house their wares. The main thoroughfare in Atlanta's business district, Whitehall Street, later renamed Peachtree Street, contained one intact block that had escaped destruction during the war. A few buildings that were salvaged from other parts of the city were moved to this block, such as jeweler Er Lawshe's storehouse, but the overall scarcity of buildings made rent very high for someone looking to lease space and set up shop. New building materials to start a store from the ground up were even more scarce and expensive.

Despite what many people would have considered insurmountable odds for starting a successful business in a city that was witnessing so much, Morris saw only opportunity. He went to his brother William and asked for a $500 loan, the approximate earnings of an average worker over the course of two years. With this loan in hand, Morris rented a twenty- by seventy-five-foot rough-hewn log building near the railroad tracks at 36 Whitehall Street and tried his luck at running a retail business.

Part I

PARTNERSHIPS
(1867–1901)

Chapter 1

M. RICH & CO.

(1867–1877)

Morris Rich opened the doors of his little dry goods shop, M. Rich & Co., on May 28, 1867, not quite three decades after Atlanta's first store, Johnson & Thrasher, opened its doors circa 1840. Immediately, he faced stiff competition from the approximately 250 existing stores in the city, including the successful retail businesses of W.A. Moore; E.W. Marsh; C.E. Boynton & E.P. Chamberlin; M.C. & J.F. Kiser; and Charles Heinz & John Berkele. Berkele would later open Maier & Berkele jewelers. Yet what may have set Morris's store apart from its competition was the treatment of its customers from the start.

On the first day of business, it rained. Morris, who feared his potential customers might ruin their footwear by trekking through the muddy street into his store, placed boards on the ground in front of his store to provide them with easier, drier access. Also on that first day and thereafter, Morris allowed people to pay on credit. At the time, many stores only did a cash business, but Morris knew that "cash" was hard to come by after the war. Oftentimes, rural customers might only get paid once a year when their crops were harvested and sold. Therefore, Morris allowed them to buy on credit and pay him when they had been paid for their crops. He also allowed customers to barter for goods with chickens, eggs, corn and other farm produce.

Within months of the store opening, Morris had hired his first employee, his cousin Adolph Teitlebaum. By the end of the first year, Morris had hired three other salesmen. With net sales around $5,000 by the close of 1867, all

Left: A sketch of how M. Rich & Co. might have looked in 1867. This sketch has been widely used as the "standard" depiction of the first store. *Courtesy of the Kenan Research Center at the Atlanta History Center.*

Below: This view of the store from a 1917 promotional piece might be a more accurate rendition of M. Rich & Co. as it appeared when it opened on Whitehall Street (now Peachtree Street).

five employees had witnessed the women of Atlanta snatching up the store's best sellers, fifty-cent corsets and twenty-five-cent hose. Those early M. Rich & Co. employees also had witnessed, by today's standards, the strange buying habits of nineteenth-century customers. Since the Better Business Bureau and stricter government regulations on quality goods were decades away in 1867, customers were wary of the quality of the goods they were buying. They would often ravel out the edge of fabric and chew on the thread or set fire to a small scrap of the material and sniff the smoke to see if what they were buying was real wool. Too, it was not uncommon for a customer of the 1800s to expect a lagniappe, a small token gift, to be thrown into their purchase when they paid their bill.

By 1871, another cousin of Morris's, Samuel Rich, was helping customers in the Atlanta store. It was also in 1871 that Morris's brother Emanuel, who had opened a store in Albany with older brother Daniel, abandoned the

COMMISSION MERCHANT,

No. 53 Peach-Tree Street, Atlanta, Ga.

STEINHEIMER BROS.,

NEW YORK STORE,

No. 34 WHITEHALL STREET,

WHOLESALE DEALERS IN STAPLE & FANCY DRY GOODS,

BOOTS, SHOES, HATS, Etc., Etc.,

ATLANTA, - - - GEORGIA.

M. RICH & CO.,

WHOLESALE AND RETAIL DEALERS IN

STAPLE AND FANCY

DRY GOODS,

Boots, Shoes, Hats, Etc., Etc.

Chisolm's New Building, No. 36 Whitehall Street,

ATLANTA, GA.

Look out for the open-work sign across the Street.

An 1870 ad in *Hanleiter's Atlanta City Directory* touting M. Rich & Co. as a dealer of dry goods, an array of consumer goods excluding groceries and hardware items.

R. M. Rose & Co., Wines, Liquors & Cigars—5 East Broad St.

25

south Georgia town and joined Morris as a clerk in his store. Daniel would join his brothers as a clerk in the store a few years later, thereby truly making the enterprise a family one.

In these early years, Morris started to advertise his business. Barring handbills, window displays and posters hung around town, one of the first widely distributed ads on the business was in the 1870 *Atlanta City Directory*. That ad stated, "M. Rich & Co., WHOLESALE AND RETAIL DEALERS IN STAPLE AND FANCY DRY GOODS, Boots, Shoes, Hats, Etc., Etc."[2] By 1875, M. Rich & Co. had been mentioned in the *Atlanta Constitution* more than a dozen times with ads proclaiming: "Great Sale of Goods From the Great Boston Fire…100 dozen French Woven Corsets, at 65 cents each…500 dozen latest style Ladies' Linen Collars at 5 cents to 10 cents each"; "Another Slaughter of Dry Goods For Twenty Days only at M. Rich & Co.'s—We offer our splendid stock of Dry Goods…at prices that will induce the public to buy, whether they wanted them or not"; and "POSITIVELY FOR SIX DAYS ONLY… Ladies will do well to avail themselves in getting cheap goods. Go to M. Rich & Co's."[3]

Within eight years, Morris's business had exploded and as a result had outgrown its original location at 36 Whitehall Street. On July 19, 1875, the store moved to 35 Whitehall Street, and not quite two months later, on September 1, the store moved once again to 43 Whitehall Street, where it shared the building with a shoe salesman by the name of Robinson. A month later, the store moved again to the former location of fellow Atlanta retailer Peck de Saulles's store at 65 Whitehall Street. This new location provided greater exposure for M. Rich & Co., as it was on the corner of busy Hunter and Whitehall Streets.

Chapter 2

M. RICH & BRO.

(1877–1884)

In a December 1876 *Atlanta Constitution* ad, Morris Rich announced to the public that he was selling large quantities of merchandise to make room for forthcoming spring merchandise and that he was going out of the "Shoe Trade," which he never did; however, the ad contained a much bigger announcement: come February 1, Morris's brother Emanuel would be admitted to the firm's partnership, and the name of the firm would be changed from M. Rich & Co. to M. Rich & Bro.[4]

Just a year after Emanuel joined the firm as a partner and the store changed its name, M. Rich & Bro. became one of the "Big Five" retailers in the city, joining Chamberlin, Boynton & Company; John Ryan's; John Keely's; and D.H. Dougherty's, all of which were located within close proximity to each other on Whitehall Street. The leader of the Big Five, Chamberlin, Boynton & Company, was divided into three departments—dry goods, carpets and boots and shoes—a precursor to becoming a true department store, which many of the other stores would copy. Later, John Ryan's was pushed out of the Big Five by J.M. High's store, High & Herrin; High's name would later become synomonus with Atlanta's leading art museum, the High Museum of Art.

Equally important was that about the time the store became one of the Big Five, it opened a small sales room for the display of ladies' and children's ready-made dresses and underwear where *women* were employed as sales clerks. While women having jobs at this time during the nineteenth century was the exception rather than the norm, M. Rich & Bro.'s was not the first

The Rich brothers pose for a photographer in the mid-1870s. *Left to right*: Daniel, Morris and Emanuel Rich. *Courtesy of the Cuba Family Archives of The Breman Museum.*

store in Atlanta to utilize their employ. That distinction went to smaller competitor Regenstein & Kutz's. In addition to being sales clerks, women, alongside men, worked in M. Rich & Bro.'s tailoring and made-to-order facilities, which manufactured underwear and children's clothes.

In 1880, a dressmaking shop was added to M. Rich & Bro.'s store on the third floor. As ready-to-wear goods were in their infancy in the late 1870s and early 1880s, M. Rich & Bro. hoped its new shop would lure more women to the store. In advertisements that were written in the form of letters targeting women, the store touted its ability to make dresses in the latest style and sell them cheaper than any woman could buy the fabric and make comparable dresses at her home. Therefore, not only money but also time was saved by buying dresses directly off the store's sales racks.

Above: Looking south down Whitehall Street at the heart of Atlanta's retailing center in 1882.

Right: A bill of sale dated April 8, 1881, showing an image of M. Rich & Bro.'s store at the corner of Whitehall and Hunter Streets.

A Mrs. M.A. Taylor was temporarily hired in 1881 to manage the store's dressmaking department, but Morris and Emanuel knew they had to hire someone with renown to head up the department, someone they could tout as a master seamstress, dressmaker and style icon. To that end, Morris went to New York City and scouted around for a candidate. It was not long before he telegraphed Emanuel back in Atlanta: "Have engaged Madame Marie Gillette, formerly of Paris, France…Let the Ladies Know This."[5] Morris snagged Gillette from Bloom Brothers in New York City, where she had been in charge of the dressmaking and designing department. Once in Atlanta, Gillette's services and skills quickly helped M. Rich & Bro.'s dress department become the place for women to get the latest fashions from around the world, particularly fashionable New York. In addition to making the store a fashion leader in women's clothes, Gillette helped the dress department become a great money generator for the store.

Before the dress department was added, M. Rich & Bro. was well into using a "fixed-price" or "one-price" system. Items were clearly marked with a price tag, doing away with the common practice of the time of bargaining or dickering on prices for items. The store advertised in the *Atlanta Constitution*, "Send your order or your children if you can't come yourself, for we have but one price and that is the lowest. All our goods are marked in plain figures—no fancy marks."[6] Also, liberal credit and customer service policies had been established. The store would take back almost any merchandise a customer was not satisfied with, even if it was not purchased at the store, and insisted that its customers be happy with the items they purchased or their money would be refunded.

In the early 1880s, it was not just new departments and policies that were gracing M. Rich & Bro.'s premises. Brother Daniel Rich, who started at

M. Rich & Bros. store in the mid-1880s at 54–56 Whitehall Street. The store boasted of having the first plate-glass windows in Atlanta. *Courtesy of the Kenan Research Center at the Atlanta History Center.*

the store around 1878, and father Joseph Rich, who started at the store when he emigrated from Hungary in 1880, were working alongside brothers Morris and Emanuel. Ironically, William, the oldest brother, the first to settle in Atlanta and the one to loan Morris money to open his store, moved to Nashville, Tennessee, in the year between Daniel's and Joseph's employ.

In 1882, M. Rich & Bro. had outgrown its location on the corner of Whitehall and Hunter Streets. For several months, a larger location at 54 and 56 Whitehall Street had been remodeled and readied for the store to move into. On September 4, the store moved into its new location, but it was a little over a week before it was opened to the public on September 15 and 16. Upon its grand opening, the High Victorian architecturally styled store, decorated with black and gold colors and elaborate gas chandeliers inside, was heralded as the most complete store of its kind in the South. Praised, too, was the store's impressive dressmaking department under the supervision of Gillette.

Chapter 3

M. RICH & BROS.

(1884–1901)

While Daniel Rich had worked as a clerk at M. Rich & Bro. with his brothers for several years, it was not until July 1, 1884, that he was admitted into the firm's partnership. At that time, the store's name was restyled to include the addition—M. Rich & Bros.

With the three brothers running the store, duties were shared. At times, one would go and buy merchandise in New York and overseas in such places as England and France, while the others stayed behind to manage the store. Goods were arriving daily in Atlanta from these trips. What distinguished M. Rich & Bros.'s buying practices from other stores in the city was that the store did not buy shiploads of furniture, as some stores did, but bought merchandise in small lots, which allowed it to offer more types of products at a faster rate than competitors that were loaded down with large quantities of the same items. Within just a few years, the firm would hire its first New York buyer to help the brothers select and send merchandise to Atlanta.

It was also during this partnership that the store's carpet department came into its own and became lucrative. Headed by J.J. Haverty, who had previously worked at John Ryan & Co. as a clerk before starting at M. Rich & Co. in 1876, the department earned large profits by bypassing carpet wholesalers and buying directly from factories, something M. Rich & Bros.'s growing clout as a leading retailer in Atlanta helped it do.

In 1885, while still working at M. Rich & Bros., Haverty and his brother, Michael, with Morris Rich's blessings, opened Haverty Furniture Co. For four years, Haverty worked for Morris during the day and at his own store

Daniel Rich in a studio portrait taken in the 1890s. *Courtesy of the Kenan Research Center at the Atlanta History Center.*

during the night until he joined forces with A.G. Rhodes and opened Rhodes-Haverty Furniture Company on May 1, 1889. At that point, Haverty quit his job at M. Rich & Bros. and focused his efforts on building a furniture empire, which, despite going through various mergers and name changes, operates to this day as Haverty's.[7]

At the same time that Haverty was opening his own store in 1885, M. Rich & Bros. introduced its first installment plan for customers to use to purchase goods. In offering this new service, the store reiterated its stance in guaranteeing one price for all and that every article sold in the store was a first-class good, offered at a great and reasonable price. Additionally, the stature of women's roles within the store continued to grow under the new partnership. Madame Marie Gillette, who had turned the dressmaking department into a huge success a few years earlier, had been promoted to a buying position, uncommon for a woman at the time. With her duties now involving travel and merchandise selection, Gillette gave up her dressmaking responsibilities to a Mrs. R.E. Tomlinson, who ran the dressmaking department located in rooms above the store's main selling floors.

In the mid-1880s, M. Rich & Bros. continued to heavily advertise its wares in local papers, increasingly taking out larger ads, including its first block ad in 1884 and its first half-page ad in 1886. As typical of the time, ads were coarse, stating, "Great slaughter of blankets and comforts," "WE DO NOT CARRY ANY CHEAP, SHODDY TRASH" and "No half price, no New York Cost! No Humbuggery!"[8] While coarse, the firm prided itself on never attacking other merchants in its advertising, insisting, rather, on ethical, straightforward advertising. By the end of the decade, the store had run its first ad using illustrations, showing ladies' wraps from $7 to $125, and its first advertisement utilizing art.[9]

Not all ads, however, were placed for selling goods or promoting the store. In a June 16, 1887 *Atlanta Constitution* ad, M. Rich & Bros. stated that one of its employees had found a pair of gold spectacles in the store and that the owner could retrieve them by simply coming into the store and asking for them. This level of attention to a single customer would become a hallmark of the store and, decades later, endear it to thousands of patrons.

Advertising in store windows was just as important as advertising in the local papers by the middle of the decade. What really helped M. Rich & Bros. in window advertising was its location and the fact that it had installed plate-glass windows in its store in 1882, a first for Atlanta, when it had moved from the corner of Whitehall and Hunter Streets to its present location. The store was in the center of all the dry goods stores located on Whitehall Street, and people would have to pass it in order to visit all the other dry goods establishments in the area; thus, M. Rich & Bros. was provided the perfect opportunity to create window displays to entice customers into its store. This "enticement" played out particularly well during the Piedmont Exposition of 1887.

In town on October 18 to visit the exposition, U.S. president Grover Cleveland and his wife arrived in downtown Atlanta via train. From the train station, the president, his wife and their entourage drove right past the store on Whitehall Street, which, along with other streets in Atlanta's central business district, had been lined by 100,000 people clamoring to see the procession. Subsequently, this event, coupled with many out-of-towners visiting the exposition in general, brought lots of foot traffic into M. Rich & Bros., where souvenirs and other goods were bought. Responsible for many of the store's fanciful window displays during this time was Lucian York, who was originally hired as a bundler at the store but would end up being one of the store's leaders around the turn of the century.

With business continually growing, M. Rich & Bros. expanded its store at 54 and 56 Whitehall Street in the late winter of 1885 and the spring of 1886. On March 29, the store opened its newly expanded space with a three-day celebration. Ten thousand souvenirs were given out to customers in celebration of the expansion, which made the store the largest dry goods store in the city. Later that year on August 8, 1886, M. Rich & Bros. became one of the first stores in Atlanta to install a telephone. Telephone #418, as it was known, was not the only modern convenience being used at the store by this time; typewriters were now employed to correspond with sellers across the globe, as well as being used for general business needs. Almost a year and a half after the phone was installed, the store expanded again, adding five thousand square feet to its back and running alongside its neighbor and competitor, John Keely's.

Throughout the 1880s and into the early 1890s, M. Rich & Bros. faced stiff competition from other stores located along Whitehall Street. The store's largest competitor at the time was Chamberlin, Boynton & Company, later Chamberlin, Johnson & Company. Chamberlin would remain its biggest competitor until 1929, when M. Rich & Bros. Co. reorganized and became the lead store. Other competitors were its neighbor John Keely's, J.M. High's, D.H. Dougherty's and John Ryan's (by 1887, John Ryan's Sons). Some of these competitors, such as John Ryan's, would fail during the 1893 depression caused by the United States' Sherman Silver Act and McKinley Tariff. Yet despite the failure of some, others remained, such as Eiseman Brothers, Bass's, McConnell & James, Fetzer & Pharr and Douglas, Thomas & Davison. Douglas, Thomas & Davison would later evolve into Davison-Paxon-Stokes and be bought by Macy's in 1925, becoming Rich's biggest competitor throughout the twentieth century.

Perhaps what set M. Rich & Bros. apart from these other stores was that it catered to the middle class. Its competitors were geared toward the "carriage trade," or upper-class customers. M. Rich & Bros., however, guaranteeing everything, had items to sell to every social class—hosiery, infants' clothes, women's dresses, men's clothes, music books, novelties and interior decorations that Emanuel Rich had personally picked out in Paris and Vienna and draperies and curtains from Damascus, as well as carpet and linoleum, which the firm would install for the customer. It was during this time that the store also went into the awning business. To help keep costs down on these items, the Rich brothers bought the goods and imported them themselves, allowing them to avoid paying commissions to traveling agents and buyers, which would bump up the prices of goods.

By 1889, M. Rich & Bros.'s carpet and drapery business had become hugely successful. In February 1889, the new Georgia State Capitol was completed with its carpet and draperies provided by M. Rich & Bros., the only Georgia firm to help furnish the building. Additionally, the store was providing carpets to many prominent buildings across the state, such as the Sweet Water Park Hotel at Salt Springs, St. Simon's Island's hotel and the Oglethorpe Hotel in Brunswick, Georgia.

In 1890, the firm expanded its carpet and drapery departments into spaces on Hunter Street behind the main store, which earned it the distinction of being the largest and most complete carpet store in the South. A year later, the store, though not yet a true department store, added a sixth new department (furniture) to its existing departments: carpet; drapery; art goods and bric-a-brac; dry goods; and art and fancy goods. It was also in 1891 that Emanuel Rich, the store's carpet buyer, and S.B. Jackson, the store's furniture buyer, negotiated with eastern and western manufacturers to create a new line of furniture exclusively for M. Rich & Bros. Within a short period of time, architects and builders would commission the store to provide carpets, draperies and furniture for their projects, such as the builders did for architect Gottfried L. Norrman's Windsor Hotel in Americus, Georgia, which was being constructed in 1891 and officially opened in June 1892. By the close of 1892, M. Rich & Bros. was selling a vast amount of furniture to hotels, offices, boardinghouses and homes throughout Atlanta and the state.

Starting in 1881 and lasting through the mid-1890s, the City of Atlanta was trying to promote itself as an industry powerhouse to the world, demonstrating how far it had come in rebuilding its industries since the American Civil War. To do this and showcase the city's, as well as the South's, trade and industrial might, many expositions, or world fairs, were held. M. Rich & Bros. was involved with these not only behind the scenes—such as Emanuel Rich's involvement as a director for the 1887 Piedmont Exposition, which attracted U.S. president Grover Cleveland—but also in the actual showcase of trade at them. In 1890, at yet another Piedmont Exposition, M. Rich & Bros. won eight medals and twenty-five dollars for its display of goods, which included oriental and decorated chinaware, Bisque and Parian ware, fancy lamps, trimmings, carpets, rugs, draperies and statuary consisting of lions and busts.

The most famous exposition ever held in Atlanta, however, was the 1895 Cotton States and International Exposition, where once again Emanuel Rich served as a director. About 800,000 people from all over the United States and thirteen foreign countries visited the event, where Booker T. Washington gave his famous "Atlanta Exposition" speech, Buffalo Bill and his Wild West Show entertained crowds and John Philip Sousa conducted his

Store employees gathered around selling tables, circa mid- to late 1890s. Morris Rich stands second from left, while Daniel Rich stands to the left of the column in the foreground.
Courtesy of the Manuscript, Archives and Rare Book Library, Emory University, Richard H. Rich papers.

"King Cotton" march, which had been penned for the occasion. Exposition participants also marveled at Kinetoscope films projected by C. Frances Jenkins and Thomas Armat's Phantascope and saw President Grover Cleveland and Ohio governor and future U.S. president William McKinley walking about the fairgrounds. Unfortunately, the event was so extravagant that the City of Atlanta went into the red—about $100,000—hosting it. To the city's good fortune, however, M. Rich & Bros. and other Atlanta businessmen and leaders came to its aid and paid off the debts.

Two years later, M. Rich & Bros., billing itself as "The Southern Emporium of Fashion," was thriving and doing business under its philosophies of "Upright dealings in all transactions," "Reliability is our trade-mark" and practicing the golden rule with its customers. The three Rich brothers were traveling to New York City, Philadelphia, London and Paris on frequent buying trips to obtain the latest in fashion and merchandise for their Atlanta customers. Once these goods were back and sold in Atlanta, the store was using two one-horse wagons, one for the north of town and one for the south of town, to deliver them directly to the consumers' doorstep. With things going so well, no one expected the sudden tragedy that befell the Rich family on the morning of Friday, July 16, 1897.

At six o'clock that morning at the private residence of Emanuel Rich on South Pryor Street, his chambermaid, Belle Scott, who was going about her morning duties, tried to enter the home's bathroom. As the door was shut, she pushed on it but found it difficult to open. Pushing on the door harder, she finally got it open to reveal Emanuel Rich bloody and unresponsive in a kneeling position on the floor. Panicked, she ran to a bedroom and woke Emanuel's wife, Bertha. Bertha ran to Emanuel and found that he was not just kneeling, wounded and ill; he was dead.

Immediately, Bertha called the family doctor, who came to the home and confirmed the death. Shortly after his arrival, the city coroner came to the home, investigated the scene and reported to those present his findings: Emanuel Rich, stabbing himself thirty-three times with a fruit knife—two wounds fatal, one puncturing the heart and the other severing the jugular vein—had committed suicide.

According to further inquiry and testimony from the physician and family, it was revealed that Emanuel Rich had been suffering from "nervous trouble"

Emanuel Rich as he appeared a few years before his 1897 suicide at age forty-eight.

and depression for months. Three weeks prior, he had gone to New York for rest but had returned to Atlanta six days before his death. The Thursday before he took his life, he dined with his brother Daniel and family but was unusually quiet and reserved throughout the meal. Afterward, he returned to his home but was nervous, so the family doctor came and gave him some opiates. Around 4:00 a.m. that Friday morning, Emanuel finally fell asleep, and his wife soon thereafter. Two hours later, he was dead. Two days later, forty-eight-year-old Emanuel's funeral was held at the home where he had taken his life.

After the untimely death of Emanuel Rich, M. Rich & Bros. continued on under the leadership of Morris and Daniel Rich, along with the assistance of Lucian York, the store's noted window decorator, and David H. Strauss, who started in 1893 at the store as an accountant. Both had been groomed for administrative jobs for years. York would eventually become a general manager and Strauss a vice-president of the store. All four led the store, which by century's end was the leading retailer in Atlanta, into the twentieth century.

Part II

M. RICH & BROS. CO. (1901–1929)

Chapter 4

MERCHANT PRINCES INCORPORATED

(1900s and 1910s)

On December 14, 1900, executive members of M. Rich & Bros. met to discuss incorporating the store to ease some of the financial strain off its partners and to allow for expansion beyond that which could be done with the accrual of annual profits. On December 20, 1900, Morris, Daniel and William Rich; Emanuel Rich's widow, Bertha; and David Strauss filed a petition for a charter of incorporation, which was granted on January 12, 1901. At a January 18, 1901 stockholder meeting, the new management structure of the store was decided. Morris was elected president and Daniel vice-president and treasurer of the store, while William and Strauss were installed as members of its board of directors. Thus, the store completed its conversion from a partnership into a company.

Now billing itself as M. Rich & Bros. Co., the newly minted company ventured into new territory. First up was its 1901 venture into the mail-order business on a wide scale, which the company boasted about in its spring and summer catalogue distributed that April. Catalogue customers could use their redeemable Star and Crescent trading stamps, issued with the catalogues, to purchase items and were offered refunds and exchanges on merchandise just as in-store customers were. Within three years, this business was booming, with approximately twenty thousand catalogues mailed to customers throughout the South.

Also new that year was M. Rich & Bros. Co.'s greatly expanded furniture store. At fifty by eighty-six feet of space on each of its five floors, the new furniture department offered bedroom, dining room, parlor, library, hall and

A decade after M. Rich & Bros. entered the furniture business in 1891, the store touted the expansion with banners along Whitehall Street. *Courtesy of the Manuscript, Archives and Rare Book Library, Emory University, Richard H. Rich papers.*

The store advertised its "Rebuilding Furniture Sale" along Hunter Street in spaces it had acquired in 1890 to expand its carpet and drapery departments. *Courtesy of the Manuscript, Archives and Rare Book Library, Emory University, Richard H. Rich papers.*

office furniture from Chicago; Grand Rapids, Michigan; and Cincinnati, Ohio factories. The store had earned a stellar reputation over the years in providing furniture not only to the Georgia State Capitol and various hotels, such as the Piedmont, Hotel Aragon and Kimball House, but also to Atlanta's grand opera house, DeGive's.

More important than expanding its mail-order business and furniture offerings, however, was the fact that M. Rich & Bros. Co. became a true department store in 1901. Beaten by Bass Dry Goods Company, which two years earlier had become Atlanta's first "true" department store, M. Rich & Bros. Co. ushered in the still relatively new concept of multiple, distinct departments housed within one store, each with its own dedicated staff, to customers not so keen on the idea. Customers were used to the days of the call trade, when they could have the same salesperson wait on them throughout the entire store. Morris, assuring his customers that the new system was more efficient, persevered and saw the department store concept not only become the norm within the dry goods retailing industry but also supplant the latter as the generic term to describe his store and others like it.

Now operating as a department store, M. Rich & Bros. Co. did as it had always done and continually stressed through advertising the quality of its goods sold at fair prices and an overall appreciation of the patronage it received. Also in these early days as a department store, semiannual sales in January and July were held to clean out stock reserves in order to make room for fresh, new and exciting merchandise. By 1903, some of this new merchandise included the company's own private brands, such as "Rich's Taffeta Lawn," "Rich's Tub Cloth" and "Rich's Lingerie."

With successful sales and new products continually being added to the shelves, as well as the company's reputation for outstanding customer service, M. Rich & Bros. Co. continued to experience exponential growth. To try and keep up with this growth, the company remodeled and expanded several times between 1903 and 1905; however, it was soon realized that simple additions and remodels would not provide a permanent solution. Therefore, from April to December 1906, the company literally rebuilt, expanded, remodeled and reorganized its current location from the ground up. During these nine months of construction, the store was open, but merchandise and customers constantly scuttled from one location to the next to accommodate ongoing work.

On January 12, 1907, M. Rich & Bros. Co. opened its newly remodeled and expanded store at 52, 54 and 56 Whitehall Street. The store of white

In January 1907, M. Rich & Bros. Co. opened its newly remodeled and expanded store on Whitehall Street. The white-brick building designed by Morgan & Dillon still stands and is known as The Mall at 82 Peachtree.

brick and sweeping, beveled plate-glass windows, designed by Atlanta architects Morgan & Dillon in the Chicago School or Commercial style, was heralded as metropolitan in character, perfect in design and convenient in every detail.[10]

The new store had a sixty-five-foot entrance front complete with mahogany doors and two huge show windows. Inside on the ground floor, which contained the notions, white and dress goods departments and a glove counter, customers were greeted with white colonial columns; white walls; white metal ceilings; mahogany shelves paneled at intervals with mirrors; glass display cases on green marble bases; wrapping counters hemmed into the display cases by small, paneled doors; cash registers; and telephones. From the center of the store at ground level, one could look up into a four-story atrium capped by two huge skylights, surrounded by electrical lights for

M. Rich & Bros. Co. (1901–1929)

Atlanta artist Chad Paulin's graphite sketch of the 1907 store illustrates the marquee and plate-glass windows that greeted customers at the end of the decade. *Courtesy of Chad Paulin.*

nighttime use. At the back of the store on the first level was an elevator bank with a soda fountain next to it.

From the first floor, one could take the grand staircase up to the second floor, which was devoted to the suits, cloaks and lingerie departments. Along the front of the store on this floor was a leather window seat that stretched the width of the store and matched the leather seating stretching around four forward columns. Weathered oak furnishings, draperies, large plate-glass display cases, eight fitting rooms, a ladies' restroom and parlor and executive offices completed the floor.

On the third floor, customers would find the carpets, rugs, draperies, matting and upholstering departments. Additionally, brass goods and bric-a-brac could be found here. Just above these departments, encompassing the entire fourth floor, was the furniture department. The furniture department also occupied a five-story ell to the left of the main building. Another ell on the right of the store contained the crockery, shoe and piano departments, a spot for a floral vendor, sewing rooms for altering and fitting, a telephone exchange, private offices and the advertising department.

The store's basement contained stock areas, as well as an employee restaurant and restrooms for its hundreds of workers. Completing the store at its back were two large entrance/exit arches. These two arches were connected to the city's streets by a semicircular drive capable of handling six wagons for shipping and unloading goods. Within three years, these wagons would be replaced by new Gramm delivery trucks.

Once the new store was opened, it did not stop expanding and offering more goods. In 1908, the list of departments for the store was extensive: dry goods; ready-to-wear; men's, women's and children's furnishings; hosiery; underwear; shoes; gloves and handkerchiefs; ribbons; neckwear; notions; jewelry; toilet articles; fancy goods; embroideries and laces; rugs; carpets; curtains; furniture; china; pianos; sheet music; candy; flowers; and others. Additionally, the company got into millinery goods and offered the services of three corset fitters who had all studied corset making.

Also in 1908, the mail-order department was enlarged and reorganized, as well as the shoe department, which had been moved to the main floor of the store. To help promote the new shoe salon, M. Rich & Bros. Co. gave a pair of doll shoes, free of charge, to any little girl accompanied by an adult who brought her doll with her to the store. If the store did not have any shoes in stock that fit the doll, its employees would quickly have some made up before the little girl left the premises.

Two years later on June 1, 1910, M. Rich & Bros. Co. premiered something new in Atlanta: an Economy Basement. The day before the basement opened, the company proclaimed in an *Atlanta Journal* newspaper ad: "We present another innovation—another new departure for Atlanta's largest department store—our Economy Basement 'A store within a store' for the sale of less expensive lines of merchandise."[11] Selling everything from clothing to cooking accessories, the new department was phenomenally successful and enlarged just ten months after it opened. Over the next century, it would experience several name changes and move to several different locations—the basement of the 1924 Store for Fashion and then the 1948 Store for Homes—evolving into one of the company's most beloved departments.[12]

By the end of the first decade of the twentieth century, the company was amply promoting its credit policies. While M. Rich & Bros. Co. had always offered credit to its customers in some form or fashion since 1867, and installment plans since 1885, many people, retailers and customers alike, looked down on extending or using credit to buy goods. Up until the early 1900s, most customers would save up money to purchase large items with cash. M. Rich & Bros. Co., however, and other department stores across the nation were turning these notions on their sides. For people who could not afford to purchase a large item, they were making credit an attractive way to purchase one, enjoy it immediately and pay for it over time.

M. Rich & Bros. Co. (1901–1929)

As a result of the company's promotion of its credit and installment plan policies, customers began to steadily buy furniture, appliances and pianos on credit. In particular, sewing machines became popular items purchased with credit. A Grand Union machine could be purchased for two dollars down and one dollar a week until it was paid for in full. By 1913, customers who had opened credit accounts simply flashed their "identification coins," which resembled a metal key chain with an account number on one side and the company's emblem on the other side, to complete a purchase.

In the second decade of the twentieth century, M. Rich & Bros. Co. became a business training ground of sorts. The store offered free embroidery classes to women, meeting Tuesday and Thursday mornings and Thursday afternoons, and took in local boys to train in the art of retailing. In addition to these women and boys, the store trained its own junior workers in the art of advertising, buying and selling, thus creating the opportunity for many people to advance up the store's ranks, going, perhaps, from a bundle wrapper to a general manager, as had happened with Lucian York.

M. Rich & Bros. Co. also reached out to local business organizations to offer assistance during this time. The Atlanta Merchants and Manufacturer's Association's 1912 meeting, held February 13–16, brought four to five thousand Georgia and southern businessmen to town. A guest speaker at that year's meeting was Woodrow Wilson, who five months later would clinch the Democratic nomination for president and four months after that be sworn in as the twenty-eighth U.S. president. M. Rich & Bros. Co., not wanting to pass up an opportunity to network and market itself at the same time, courted Wilson and the association through newspaper ads to use its store as their downtown "home" during the meeting's tenure. Coincidentally, Wilson had practiced law briefly in Atlanta in 1883 at the corner of Broad and Alabama Streets, which in little over a decade would become the site of M. Rich & Bros. Co.'s new store.

With Wilson elected president in 1912 on a platform to curb big business, which resulted in a recession and then a depression in 1914, coupled with the outbreak of World War I in July 1914, a perfect storm had developed to cripple Georgia's cotton production. Georgia cotton farmers had relied on Europe to purchase their cotton, thus staving off economic problems faced at home. However, within a month of the war starting, cotton markets in Europe were sealed off, and cotton was stacking up in towns all across the state. In order to prevent financial ruin for the farmers and to beat the depression locally, one hundred Atlanta businessmen launched the "Buy a Bale of Cotton" movement. One of the five members of the group's executive committee was M. Rich & Bros. Co.'s financial chief, David Strauss. Rallying behind the movement, Atlanta businesses bought 301 bales of cotton, many of which were bought by M. Rich & Bros. Co. and used as decorations throughout the store. Seventeen years later, the company would once again come to cotton farmers' aid and accept "cotton as cash," taking up 5,000 bales in exchange for merchandise.

This policy of supporting its community through philanthropic endeavors was repeatedly displayed during the mid-teens by M. Rich & Bros. Co. In 1915, the company gave $2,400 to help the city host a southeastern fair. A year later, it, along with other department stores in Atlanta, helped Emory University finance its new campus being constructed in Atlanta. A year after that, seventy-three city blocks containing over 1,500 homes were destroyed in the Great Fire of Atlanta. Morris Rich and his staff were on hand to provide clothes and household goods to those displaced. When America entered

A 1917 view of M. Rich & Bros. Co.'s main selling floor decorated to celebrate the company's fiftieth anniversary. The store's early "star and crescent" logo is present on the banner spanning the aisle. *Courtesy of the Manuscript, Archives and Rare Book Library, Emory University, Richard H. Rich papers.*

World War I that year, it was members of that same staff who knitted scarves and hosiery for servicemen overseas and sang every morning at the bottom of the main stairs after the store's doors were thrown open, "America," "Tipperary," "Keep the Home Fires Burning" and other patriotic songs.

Just a month after America had entered World War I, M. Rich & Bros. Co. celebrated its fiftieth anniversary in May 1917. While the store had previously asked customers to loan it items bought in the store twenty-five to fifty years earlier for an in-store exhibit to run the entire anniversary month, the biggest components of the celebrations were huge sales on numerous products. During the entire month, customers could purchase a ten-piece Chinese Chippendale dining room set for $225.00, originally $305.00, or purchase dresses starting at $2.49, silk stockings starting at $0.95, one of six hundred pieces of La France Ivory toiletware starting at $0.98 or many other items specially marked for the anniversary sales. The store also asked customers to do their part by purchasing knit mufflers and caps approved by the navy department and sold at the store for the brave "Jack Tars" serving on warships in the cold latitudes of Europe at that time, even though it was springtime and warm in Georgia.

A year and a half later, World War I ended, but the war for retail dominance in Atlanta continued to rage on. By 1918, Kelly Co., J.M. High Co., Davison-Paxon-Stokes Co., J.P. Allen Co., J. Regenstein, George Muse & Co. and J. Frohsin were the dominant retailing establishments challenging M. Rich & Bros. Co. for its customers and profits. The biggest retail threat

M. Rich & Bros. Co. began delivering merchandise via delivery trucks across Atlanta by 1910 and, just eight years later, owned this fleet of Ford Model Ts.

to the company, however, was Chamberlin, Johnson & DuBose Co. In 1918, Chamberlin, Johnson & DuBose moved into its new five-story building, which offered its customers an impressive restaurant to dine in on its fifth floor. The opening of this new store pushed M. Rich & Bro. Co. into second place in the retail pecking order of the city.

Recognizing that its place as the number-one retailer in Atlanta had been surpassed, M. Rich & Bros. Co. set about to regain its dominance. A year after the new Chamberlin store had opened, the company announced on August 3, 1919, that it had leased a lot on the corner of Broad and Alabama Streets. Here, a new store would rise to hopefully place M. Rich & Bros. Co. back at the top.

Chapter 5

PALACE OF COMMERCE

(1920s)

At the start of the 1920s, M. Rich & Bros. Co. was planning its new store and looking for new ways to increase the number of customers coming in the store's doors. Unfortunately, the company experienced an unexpected setback four months into the new decade with the death of Daniel Rich. Daniel had been in ill health for about a year, yet his death from arterial sclerosis on April 12, 1920, nine days before his seventy-sixth birthday, came as a shock to his family and employees at M. Rich & Bros. Co. Having worked at the company since the 1870s, been admitted into the partnership in 1884 and served as its vice-president for the past nineteen years, Daniel had become a huge factor in the growth and success of one of Atlanta's most beloved firms. He had also established himself as one of Atlanta's most prominent citizens and a huge proponent of aiding and building the city into a southern economic powerhouse.

With Daniel's death and Emanuel's suicide twenty-three years earlier, Morris was left as the sole Rich brother at the helm of the company. Moving into Daniel's position as vice-president was Emanuel's son, Walter H. Rich, who had joined the company as an employee in 1901. For a short time, Morris and Walter, along with David Strauss and Lucian York (who would die in 1924), would continue to lead the firm; however, they would soon be joined by Morris's grandson, Richard H. Rich, in 1923, Frank H. Neely in 1924 and Ben R. Gordon in 1925, all of whom would lead the firm into decades of retail dominance not only in Atlanta but also throughout the South.

Customers shopping at Rich's Curb Market during the 1960s. The event kicked off the Annual Harvest Sale, which began in the early 1920s. *Courtesy of the Manuscript, Archives and Rare Book Library, Emory University, Richard H. Rich papers.*

Back to business as usual after Daniel's death, Morris and his colleagues continued on in their efforts to once again reclaim the crown for their company as the leading retailer in Atlanta. To that end, they added to the store new sales promotions to be offered to its customers. Joining anniversary sales, stock clearance sales and holiday sales was M. Rich & Bros. Co.'s new Annual Harvest Sale. This sale was kicked off in the fall with a Curb Market, which involved turning the sidewalks in front of the store into open-air markets. At these markets, vendors included farmers selling their produce and farm goods and Home Demonstration Clubs and 4-H Clubs touting their services.

Also during this time, the company started its Thrift Thursdays sales, created sales promotions to tie into specific local events, such as a 1921 southeastern fair, and started using its "star and crescent" logo to indicate sale items throughout the store not necessarily associated with any particular event. In 1922, the store started sponsoring its Atlanta Day sales promotions, which were done twice a year and became so popular that they were considered civic occasions. Some sales events, such as the store's fifty-fifth anniversary sale in 1922, attracted the attention of famous journalists to report on them, such as the *Atlanta Journal*'s O.B. Keeler. Keeler, who was famous for reporting on Atlanta's noted golfer Bobby Jones, wrote about the anniversary sale and the events surrounding it, including a giant book in the store's street-level window display case titled the *Great Book of Atlanta*, which displayed the history of the city on pages over five feet tall.

In addition to sales, the store inaugurated new customer services, such as free daily needlework classes for the public in 1923. Despite these new sale promotions and customer services, however, it was not until the completion of M. Rich & Bros. Co.'s new department store in 1924 that the firm reasserted itself as Atlanta's greatest retailer.

Bucking the trend in Atlanta of businesses moving northward up Peachtree Street, the store's leaders commenced plans in the early 1920s

The M. Rich & Bros. Co. building, designed by Hentz, Reid & Adler and opened in 1924, as seen a year later at the corner of Broad and Alabama Streets. *Photo by Robert D. Klein, courtesy of the Kenan Research Center at the Atlanta History Center.*

to build a grand new department store one block north and one block west of their old store at the corner of Broad and Alabama Streets. By 1922, construction had begun on the new store, whose footprint when completed would cover the site of fourteen previous storefronts along not only Broad and Alabama Streets but also Forsyth Street. The store's impressive 421 feet of show window frontage would make it the largest department store south of Philadelphia.

Completed by the spring of 1924, the store was designed by Hentz, Reid and Adler in the Italian Renaissance or Renaissance Revival style. Its exterior of Indiana limestone, beige bricks, double-hung sash windows on its upper floors and large display windows at street level were accentuated with rusticated surrounds, prominent keystones, ornate broken pediments, limestone arches, pilasters, swags and intricate iron and glass marquees. The building's focal point, however, was its forty-five-degree beveled angle at the Broad-Alabama Street corner. Here, limestone scaled the full height of the building, and just above an arched display window, a clock sat within an ornate cartouche at the second-floor level. The clock, which would become

Rich's famous clock, set in an elaborate cartouche on a corner of the store, inspired Oliver F. Reeves, poet laureate of Georgia from 1944 to 1963, to write the poem "The Clock on the Corner." *Courtesy of Thomas Asher.*

a revered symbol of Rich's, was not, ironically, included in the original architectural plans of the building. Instead, the spot was to have housed an ornate wrought-iron grille.

The interior of the store showcased entry vestibules with variegated green marble benches, which opened up onto the main selling floor of the store. There, plaster ceilings, decorative columns, classical moldings, walnut paneling and woodwork with gold trimmings, marble floors and glass display cabinets extended to a back wall containing a bank of five elaborately decorated elevators. Unlike the previous store, this one contained no central stairwell.

Above the main selling floor was a mezzanine that ran the full length of Broad and Alabama Streets. Above that were floors two through six, which contained selling space, storage space, department offices, a kitchen and restaurant and an elaborate suite of pine-paneled executive offices that included the Chart Room, an executive meeting space tucked into the fifth-floor beveled edge of the building. Rounding out the building were a partial subbasement, basement and shipping and receiving area.

A modern view of the limestone detailing around the upper portion of one of the two main entrances at M. Rich & Bros. Co.'s 1924 store.

Dubbed by the press as "Rich's Palace of Commerce" and the "South's Greatest Department Store," the store's official grand opening was held March 24, 1924. That day, however, no merchandise of any kind was sold at the store. Instead, Atlantans were asked to simply come to the new $1.5 million, 180,000-square-foot "palace" and partake of the opening day festivities, which included fashion shows, orchestral presentations and speeches from the likes of Georgia governor Clifford Walker, Atlanta mayor Walter Sims, pioneer druggist and the first purveyor of Coca-Cola Dr. Joseph Jacobs and other politicians, businessmen and civic leaders. Also on hand to greet the throngs of spectators were store executives, including the store founder, seventy-seven-year-old Morris Rich, who was standing in a store one hundred times larger than the one he had started fifty-seven years earlier.[13]

The following day, the store officially opened for "business." Customers had seventy-five complete departments to stroll through, as well as the opportunity to take advantage of six new services: the "Ask Mr. Foster" Travel Information Service, a free-of-charge travel agent; Rich's Home Service, an expert interior decorator available to help customers with their decorating needs, including calculating costs of new furniture, rugs and draperies; a tearoom, which offered white customers only a la carte dishes and beverages for consumption or a place for their clubs to gather for meetings and luncheons during the week; a "Quest of Beauty" service led by Kathleen Mary Quinlan of New York City, who offered women free beauty tips; an exclusive dressmaking salon run by Madame Yvonne of Paris; and new, larger restrooms with easy chairs for relaxing.

Now once again at the top of the retail pecking order in Atlanta, M. Rich & Bros. Co. promised its customers that no transaction would be closed until complete satisfaction had been obtained, to have greater services and value in goods than any other store could give, to have every courtesy a modern department store could offer in the most comfortable and safest store with the most convenience to be found anywhere and to have the earliest access to the latest fashions, furniture and goods from all over the world. The company also asked its customers to place their confidence in it as a retail leader and to offer it any chance to correct any faults perceived of the store so that they could be corrected in order to provide better service.[14] It is with these promises and commitments to its customers that the company began to add additional perks and services to its new store.

First added was a nursery in 1925. Founded by the company's trained nurse, Jean Wallace, a native of Firth of Clyde, Scotland, who was assisted by Mrs. Alma, a black employee, the nursery became a place where women could drop off their children ages six months to six years, free of charge, while they went about the store shopping, unencumbered with children in tow. Children in the nursery could play with toys and games, as well as ride a four-car, self-propelled merry-go-round. Located in the center of the nursery and operating from 9:00 a.m. to 5:00 p.m. every day, the merry-go-round would become a cherished memory for many of Atlanta's children as it, as well as the nursery, ran for decades.

In addition to the nursery, M. Rich & Bros. Co. added in 1925 what would become one of its most generous and longest-lasting services for its customers: Penelope Penn. Customers, however, were not the only ones getting new services that year. M. Rich & Bros. Co.'s over eight hundred employees were introduced to one of their longest-lasting services, *Rich Bits*.

PENELOPE PENN

When M. Rich & Bros. Co.'s new store opened in 1924, store executives secured the services of the Junior League of Atlanta in staging a fashion show. In charge of the show were prominent Junior League members and Atlanta socialites Mrs. Lott Warren Jr. and Mrs. Eugene Harrington.[15] So impressed was M. Rich & Bros. Co. with the success of the show and the capabilities of its leaders that the store offered them both permanent positions at the store. Warren went on to be the assistant to the manager of the store's interior decorating department. Harrington, on the other hand, went on to head a service that would become legendary not just in Atlanta but throughout the country—Penelope Penn, a free, personal service bureau.

No one knows who came up with Penelope Penn first, Harrington or an executive at the company, but what is known is that when Saks Fifth Avenue opened in New York in 1924, it had hired blueblood society matron Morgan Belmont to head its personal-shopping department, which had quickly become a great success. Either store executives or Harrington knew of this, and perhaps one or the other, or both, decided to copy that success in Atlanta.[16]

In a January 28, 1925 *Atlanta Constitution* article, M. Rich & Bros. Co. touted: "The constant aim of this store is to be of greater service to the public! To this end, we have established a 'Personal Service Bureau' under the expert direction and personal supervision of an experienced woman, Miss Penelope Penn. There is no service too great, none too small, for her to give you. Free of charge, of course!"[17] When opened, the bureau had two employees, Harrington and one other.

M. Rich & Bros. Company

PENELOPE PENN

RICH'S Personal Service~

Signed

Penelope Penn

Penelope Penn answers customers' questions in Ann Landers style in this 1925 newspaper advertisement. *Courtesy of Macy's, Inc.*

M. Rich & Bros. Co. (1901–1929)

Originally, the bureau was established to assist shoppers, mainly, in the purchasing of goods, but Penelope Penn soon offered much more. By visiting the bureau in the actual store or by ringing up "WAlnut 4636" and asking for "Penelope Penn," the service bureau also shipped items from the store to customers across the country or locally; planned trips abroad with the assistance of the store's Ask Mr. Foster travel bureau; bought theater tickets and steamship tickets; planned teas, dances and parties; booked hotel reservations; arranged taxi service; and even called a fire engine to report somewhere, all free of charge for customers. Penelope Penn even had a list of birthdays and anniversaries of store patrons and called them at their homes to remind them of the impending date and to help with selecting merchandise for the occasion.

Additionally, the service doled out Ann Landers–type advice to patrons of the store in person, by phone or by letter. The bureau often reprinted this advice in weekly newspaper columns. The questions asked ranged from "Where can I get a list of Canadian hay fever resorts?"; "Would flesh georgette do for a wedding?"; and "I love her, but she does not care for me. What should I do?" to the comical "On what floor will I find the basement, please?" and "How can I say 'I love you' on a gift card without coming right out and saying it?"

One of the first big social functions the Penelope Penn bureau was involved with was Fort Valley, Georgia's fourth annual Peach Festival, which was held March 19–20, 1925. M. Rich & Bros. Co., through Penelope Penn, procured a contract for the festival whereby the store provided 1,500 costumes, including shoes, hose and flowers, to be paraded by a cast of approximately one hundred in a fifteen-episode show on the festival's main stage. Penelope Penn's involvement with the festival worked out quite well for Harrington, as she also was the chaperone for the two Atlanta debutantes, Miss Louise Nelson and Miss Rebecca Ashcraft, representing Atlanta in Fort Valley that year.

Another unique feature of the Penelope Penn department was its library. What started out as a book-exchange service had by 1926 blossomed into a full-fledged circulating library. In 1928, when the Penelope Penn department was moved to the sixth floor next to the store's new bookshop, the library went with it. The store provided comfortable chairs and a reading nook grouped about a quaint fireplace for people to read books checked out of the library or that they had just purchased. In 1929, a Junior Circulating Library was added. Over the years, authors were invited to the store for book signings, and by the late 1930s and early 1940s, Penelope Penn was interviewing some of these authors and others, as well as giving book reviews on its weekly radio program, which several local stations broadcasted, including WSB and WGST.

By the 1940s, the library was simply called Rich's Library, where each of its books was covered with green covers, the store's trademark color, with "Rich's" embossed in gold across it. At that time, customers could borrow books for two cents a day, get a fifty-cent vacation special that included checking out six books for two weeks or buy a life membership for one dollar. And by the early 1960s, the library was offering not only books to be checked out but also a literary guild and magazine subscription service.

By the mid-1960s, the Penelope Penn bureau, without the library, had been relocated to the mezzanine level of the Store for Homes and had upward of thirty employees. At this time, Penelope Penn was directing the activity of Rich's Bride's Bureau, where they helped brides with everything from registering for silver and china, selecting wedding invitations and picking out bride's and bridesmaids' dresses to actually planning entire wedding ceremonies. Additionally, a few of the employees in the department traveled to actual customer weddings, whether they were in Atlanta or neighboring states, to help with last-minute alterations or securing the bride's veil.

After Federated Department Stores, Inc. bought Rich's in 1976, Penelope Penn's services to customers became more limited. While still assisting customers with what types of gifts to buy, answering questions about the store and assisting customers in general, the service moved more to filling customer telephone orders and operating as a corporate gift drive service, which helped large companies find and secure gifts for senior executives or company anniversaries. Eventually, even the gift service became less demanding on the department as companies chose less and less physical merchandise and moved more toward gift card giving.

With the close of Rich's flagship store in downtown Atlanta in 1991, Penelope Penn's offices and services, company-wide, were shuttered. The name Penelope Penn, however, was used up until at least the mid-1990s for advertising purposes, often being listed as the department someone could write to for warranty information on a specific product.

RICH BITS

Though officially credited by M. Rich & Bros. Co. as beginning in 1925 and having that year referenced as the start date for volume one on subsequent publications, the company's new, store-wide newsletter, *Rich Bits*, actually began publication almost exactly six months after its March 24, 1924 store opening. The first edition, printed September 25, 1924, was a simple, typed, two-page format and did not bear an official name. On October 2, 1924, a second edition of the newsletter was printed and now bore in its masthead the name *Rich Bits*.

From 1925 to 1936, *Rich Bits* appeared intermittently, but by June 1936, the publication had been revamped and began to appear regularly for Rich's more than one thousand employees. In the publication, a column titled "Office Gab" kept employees notified of events happening within the store, as well as the personal events of its employees. Poems written by staff would often appear within the pages of the newsletter, commenting on not only "young love" between two employees but on the fact that employees had no time clocks to punch and no special entrances to walk through, as was the case at many other department stores across the country. Additionally, *Rich Bits* had columns describing the recent activities on each floor of the

Rich Bits publications, such as this spring 1972 edition, informed store employees about happenings within the Rich's community for over sixty-three years. *Courtesy of Macy's, Inc.*

store, anniversary announcements, a "Colored Bits" column describing the happenings of the store's black personnel and columns over the years updating personnel of their coworkers or those coworkers' family members who were serving in World War II, the Korean War or the Vietnam War.

Over time, *Rich Bits* morphed from a simple "newsletter" style to a full-fledged magazine. Colorful covers and graphics greeted the reader, particularly in the *Rich Bits* Christmas editions. By the 1960s, these Christmas issues were often packed with stories on the Pink Pig(s), The Great Tree, Santa's Secret Shop and Operation Reindeer. In 1961, *Rich's Bits* was desegregated, as white and black employees were intermingled within its pages rather than blacks being relegated to a few pages in the back.

The latter part of the 1970s brought huge changes to *Rich Bits*. In 1976, *Rich Bits* was being styled as *Richbits*, and the once colorful, multi-paged publications had dwindled down to two or three pages in length. It also was in this year that Rich's became a division of Federated Department Stores, Inc. The store no longer being family controlled but now part of a large corporation was reflected within the pages of *Richbits*. Stories of whimsy and personnel accolades were replaced with bulletin-type, to-the-point company policy issues and stories on clothing styles and textures, as well as inventory shortage control.

After more than sixty-three years, *Richbits*, formerly *Rich Bits*, came to its end in 1988. That year, Canadian Robert Campeau took over Federated and merged Goldsmith's of Memphis with Rich's. The combined division, Rich's/Goldsmith's, created a new newsletter, *focal point*, for its joint employees.

During *Rich Bits'* heyday, the publication was joined by many other Rich's publications to help keep employees up to date with the latest news: *Rich's News Bits*, about store news; *Rich's Update*, a biweekly newsletter with tidbits about jobs, etc.; *Money Matters*, Rich's Credit Union's newsletter; and *SR.*, Rich's retiree newsletter that was delivered with pension checks.

Although the new 1924 store was opened and an immediate success and offered new services never before seen in Atlanta, M. Rich & Bros. Co.'s regained dominance of the city's retail scene was always to be a tenuous one. In 1925, a year after the new store opened, the company's chief competitor was still Chamberlin, Johnson & DuBose Co., which six years later would be a casualty of the Depression. J.P. Allen's, Regenstein's, Davison-Paxon-Stokes and Highs, which that year would be acquired by W.H. Britain and G.C. Jones, also were still around and vying for Atlantans' business. The biggest threat, however, to M. Rich & Bros. Co. over the next couple of years was the entrance of national retailers Macy's and Sears onto the Atlanta retail scene.

On June 14, 1925, Davison-Paxon-Stokes announced its official affiliation with R.H. Macy & Co. With the purchase of Davison-Paxon-Stokes, the venerable New York City retailer gained access to Atlanta and the Southeast and started a rivalry between itself and M. Rich & Bros. Co. that would last for almost eight decades until the two stores were merged. In 1927, less than two years after acquiring Davison-Paxon-Stokes, Macy's opened a new 402,531-square-foot, $7 million store under the Davison-Paxon-Stokes nameplate on Peachtree Street nine blocks north of Atlanta's central business district. While Macy's name was not over the door until 1985, its merchandise, policies and affiliations were made known in the store and in newspaper ads immediately. Also known immediately was that M. Rich & Bros. Co. had, once again, lost its claim as the largest department store south of Philadelphia.

Almost six months after Davison-Paxon-Stokes and Macy's announced their alliance, M. Rich & Bros. Co. and Atlantans got word of yet another national retailer coming to town. On December 9, 1925, Sears, Roebuck & Co. announced plans to open its ninth department store in the country in Atlanta. The new $3 million, nine-story store and mail-order department was slated to open on Ponce de Leon Avenue in August 1926. Not only was Sears another competitor, but also its decision (as well as Macy's) to build a store outside of Atlanta's central business district was a departure for retailers that generally built downtown stores. This trend would, decades later, ultimately leave M. Rich & Bros. Co.'s downtown store in an undesirable location.

Not long after the announcement of Macy's and Sears entering Atlanta, there was a change in management at M. Rich & Bros. Co. Fifty-nine years after founding the store and twenty-five years after beginning to serve as its president, Morris Rich relinquished day-to-day control of his company.

At a January 20, 1926 board of directors meeting, seventy-nine-year-old Morris was promoted to chairman of the board, while his nephew, Walter Rich, was elected president, David Strauss was elected vice-president and treasurer and Frank Neely was elected secretary and maintained his general manager title. Also elected to the company's board of directors were Richard Rich, Sol Rubin, Fred A. Sheram and J.P. Flynn. All of these directors worked at the company in various capacities.

M. Rich & Bros. Co.'s new president, Walter Rich, known by the company's staff as "Mister Walter," had spent his life learning about the retail business from his father, Emanuel, until his unfortunate suicide a couple of months after Walter's seventeenth birthday, and from his uncles, Morris and Daniel. After attending and graduating from Columbia University, Walter had returned to Atlanta and started working at M. Rich & Bros. Co. as a clerk at the wash goods counter in 1901 and then quickly rose through the company's ranks.

As was typical of all the leaders of M. Rich & Bros. Co., Walter would not only lead the day-to-day operations of the store but also would devote much of his time to serving on the boards of various organizations, such as the Atlanta Board of Education, the Atlanta Music Festival Association, Young Harris College's board of trustees, the State Board of Education and Emory University's board of trustees. He also was an active leader in several clubs, including the Standard and Progressive Clubs, and served as the director of the Trust Company of Georgia and as a trustee of The Temple. What the general public did not know, however, was that in his free time Walter enjoyed farming and could be seen on his thirty-one-acre farm at 330 Argonne Drive, now part of Buckhead Atlanta, wearing bib overalls and a straw hat, plowing fields behind his two mules, Chewing Gum and Madame Queen. This love of gardening and the outdoors eventually led Walter to establish the Dogwood Festival in 1936 to celebrate the beautiful spring season in Atlanta, an event still popular today.

Unfortunately, before Morris would see Walter serve on many of these boards or create Atlanta's Dogwood Festival, Morris died of a heart attack at eighty-one years old on June 29, 1928, while vacationing in Atlantic City with his wife, Maud, daughter, Rosalind Rosenheim, and her son and Morris's grandson, Richard Rich. Morris had been in ill health for several months before his death, and it is speculated that he stepped down as president of M. Rich & Bros. Co. two years earlier due to health reasons. The day after his death, his body was shipped via train to Atlanta, while the store he founded remained closed for the day in his honor. Following an 11:00 a.m. funeral at the chapel of Sam Greenberg & Co. on Sunday, July 1, Morris's body was interred in Atlanta's Oakland Cemetery.

Morris Rich, Atlanta's greatest merchant prince, lived to see his tiny store founded by the railroad tracks in the ruins of the city after the American Civil War grow from first-year sales of $5,000 to revenues of over $7.3 million the year before he died.

Part III

RICH'S, INC.— FAMILY CONTROLLED (1929–1976)

Chapter 6

MONEY MATTERS

(1930s)

Less than a year after Morris's death, M. Rich & Bros. Co. announced in its April 1, 1929 board of directors' minutes that the company was being reorganized. Starting that month, the merchandising business of the company was incorporated as Rich's, Inc., which would offer stock to the public for the first time, while a new and separate venture named M. Rich & Bros. Co. would operate as a real estate company, securing in future years property on which the company could expand. The everyday operations of Rich's, Inc. would be handled as had been decided in 1926—Walter Rich as president, David Strauss (who would die in 1936) as vice-president and Frank Neely as general manager.

Ironically, the management at Rich's could not have predicted that six months later, starting with Black Tuesday on October 29, the stock market would crash and plunge the United States into its worst economic recession, the Great Depression. Over the next several years, Rich's and other merchants across the country were tremendously affected by several government-imposed programs, such as the New Deal, the National Recovery Act or National Industrial Recovery Act (NIRA) and Social Security, which together put restrictions on retailers on the length of time employees were allowed to work, required increased minimum wages in some places and required the payment of additional taxes. Rich's and many stores, however, responded quickly and favorably to the new programs, generally wanting to answer U.S. president Franklin D. Roosevelt's call to provide a united front against economic depression, and established themselves as Blue Eagle employers, working within established government programs to get workers back on the job.

Ultimately, many of these government programs were deemed unconstitutional, but Rich's ever-present policy of being a community leader, especially during emergencies and difficult times, coupled with the store's cash reserves from profitable years before the Great Depression, helped it not only weather the period relatively unscathed but also allowed it to provide assistance to the Atlanta community during the difficult recession. One such assistance offered by the store, the decision to accept city-issued scrip as cash, would garner Rich's devoted, loyal, lifelong customers and would elevate the store to almost mythical status as an esteemed southern institution, sincerely interested in and committed to the southern community it served.

As a result of the stock market crash and ensuing economic depression of the 1930s, city governments, politicians, businesses and others had to find creative ways to pay employees when they had no cash to do so. Cities such as Chicago, Detroit and Atlanta were experiencing cash shortages and, therefore, issued their teachers and municipal workers scrip, a promissory note of sorts, which looked much like a bond certificate and was about the size of a dollar bill. It was hoped that the scrip would be accepted by local merchants as an alternative to cash and that once city coffers had been replenished, it would be reimbursed with real greenbacks.

Many merchants, however, were leery of accepting scrip, fearing they would be left with worthless pieces of paper. Therefore, many outright refused to accept it as payment, often telling customers to come back to their store when they had cash. If a retailer did choose to accept it for payment, they would often demand a markup from 10 to 25 percent and would often refuse to give change back in cash, only offering store credit instead.

In December 1930, when Walter Rich and Frank Neely learned that Atlanta's city council could not pay teachers' salaries for the month and was offering them scrip, the two came up with a plan to ensure that the teachers could get cash in time for Christmas. They quickly informed the city council that Rich's would cash the teachers' scrip at face value and would not require any purchase from the store in order to do so. Within days, the store had set up five booths on its fifth floor to facilitate the exchange of scrip for cash and, by December 20, had paid out over $260,000 to 1,500 teachers. Local papers boasting of Rich's acceptance of the scrip led to increased Christmas sales and turned Walter into a local hero. Many teachers who could pay their rent and buy groceries that month became, along with their families, loyal customers to the store and turned the event into local lore over ensuing years.

What often has been lost in history, however, is that the acceptance of scrip by Rich's was not simply a one-time event. The store, whose efforts caused Coca-Cola, Davison-Paxon-Stokes and other Atlanta businesses to follow suit, accepted scrip at least six other times over the following seven years, paying out during that time over half a million dollars to Atlanta teachers.

In addition to offering a helping hand to those in need during the 1930s, Rich's created new services within its store for its customers, such as its Rich's College Board. This board consisted of college-aged employees who went about informing incoming college freshman what was appropriate and newly in vogue to wear at local schools. In 1935, the store also created a service for the general public, the Garden Center of Atlanta. This non-commercial center located on the store's sixth floor acted as a headquarters for hundreds of Atlanta garden clubs, offering free garden information to those club members, as well as the public. The Garden Center also sponsored lectures on various gardening topics throughout the state and held a tulip show in the spring and a gladiolus show in the summer. For

The uncharacteristically modern seventh and partial eighth floors added to the top of Rich's in the 1930s included an employees' recreational playground, replete with deck chairs and shuffleboard courts. *Courtesy of Special Collections and Archives, Georgia State University Library.*

forty-seven years, the center operated at Rich's until it was moved in 1982 to the Atlanta Botanical Garden.

Also in 1935, the company announced that it would embark on a $350,000 expansion, and for the next two years this expansion, as well as overall improvements to the store, were carried out. The third floor was rearranged and modernized, becoming a fashion floor containing thirteen specialized shops. The sixth floor had an auditorium and meeting rooms added to it, while windows throughout the entire store were enclosed with glass blocks as air conditioning was added to the store. The largest part of the expansion, however, consisted of an uncharacteristically modern seventh and partial eighth floor added to the store by the architectural firm of Hentz, Adler & Shutze. This addition, which involved removing the store's 1924 cornice and adding two new elevators to the store's existing elevator count, included merchandise space, outdoor display rooms and an employees' recreational playground, which within the next decade would be expanded to include twelve shuffleboard courts, two hundred deck chairs, vending machines and a snack bar.

While the store had expanded during the mid- to late 1930s, cash was still tight, and obtaining credit was difficult for its customers and employees alike. To help, Rich's implemented two new programs—one to ease the financial hardships of its employees and the other to ease the financial hardships of its customers.

In 1938, Joseph F. Asher, who started at Rich's in 1921 as a shirt salesman and eventually worked his way up through the company to become a director and the vice-president and corporate secretary in charge of several merchandising divisions, had been at an industry meeting in New York where he met with Abraham "Lincoln" Filene about Filene's department store's recently opened credit union. Lincoln's brother, Edward Filene, who had died the year before, was considered the "father" of American credit unions and had helped establish national legislation to regulate credit unions across the country. Enamored by the service Filene's credit union provided to its employees and the credit union's overall success, Asher returned to Atlanta and proposed to Frank Neely that Rich's start one of its own. Neely approved the idea, and within the year, Rich's opened its own employee credit union. Started with the idea to help employees save money, allow the store an organized way to loan money to its employees rather than advancing salaries and help put an end to employees going to loan sharks for quick cash (a common practice in the 1930s), Rich's Credit Union, with Asher as its president, was an immediate success. Its coffers aided Rich's employees not only during the Depression but for decades later.

Buying items on credit became easier for Rich's customers in the late 1930s when the store introduced charga-plates, a precursor to the modern credit card. *Courtesy of Amber L'Amie Stephan.*

It was also at this time that Rich's introduced charga-plates for its customers. Created in 1928 by the Farrington Manufacturing Company of Boston, a former jewelry and eyeglass case manufacturer that had expanded into the development of credit cards and imprinters, charga-plates were 2½-inch by 1¼-inch metal plates that resembled military dog tags. The front of these plates were embossed with a customer's name and address, while the back contained a spot for a paper card printed with the issuer's name, such as "Rich's," and a signature line for the credit account holder. At the time of purchase, a customer would hand his or her plate to the sales clerk, who would then place the plate into a slot on an imprinting machine, where the customer's name and address would be imprinted by ink onto a sales slip. This sped up and simplified service at the register and greatly reduced errors in spelling and address inaccuracies for delivery purposes. On the back end in the credit and accounting departments, the sales slip would be matched to the customer's credit account and a bill produced and mailed out.

Originally, Rich's issued charga-plates exclusively for its in-store purchases; however, in June 1940, Rich's would join Allen's, High's and Davison-Paxon's in a joint effort to allow shoppers to use one plate for accounts at all four stores. This new service would be chartered under the name of the Atlanta Charga-Plate Group and function under the supervision of the Credit Service Exchange office in Atlanta.

Perhaps one of the most famous individuals to have a charga-plate account at Rich's over the following decades was First Lady Mamie Eisenhower. At the request of her good friend Nell Hodgson Woodruff, Coca-Cola magnate Robert Woodruff's wife, Eisenhower's account was opened on March 12, 1956. Woodruff had gone to Rich's to purchase for Eisenhower some draperies—three pairs of yellow curtains and a pair of floral ones. The curtains, which cost $73.92, were packaged and picked up at the store by the FBI, which then sent them to Washington, D.C. Eisenhower, who later returned the floral curtains, received her official charga-plate a few days later at the White House via mail.

After more than a quarter of a century of use, charga-plates would give way to the modern plastic credit card. However, at the close of the 1930s, a decade and a half before Eisenhower would have a Rich's charge account and decades before the advent of plastic charge cards, people were still struggling with the harsh economic times of the lingering Depression. Acting perhaps as a brief respite and diversion from these tough times in Atlanta was the premiere of the "new science" of television.

In April 1939, television had been demonstrated for the first time by RCA/NBC to crowds at New York's World Fair. A few months later, Atlanta would join New York, Chicago, Pittsburgh and San Francisco as the only U.S. cities to display for the general public this new marvel in science and entertainment. And as a leading establishment in Atlanta, it was Rich's that was chosen to display this new technology for the first time in the South.

In preparation for the event, technicians from RCA Victor Company of Camden, New Jersey, constructed in Rich's tearoom on the sixth floor a glass-paneled telecasting studio and an adjoining, darkened studio. The darkened studio contained six television sets, the largest at 12.7 inches, which crowds would gather around to watch the events that were being televised from the glass-paneled studio next door. RCA's technicians were assisted by staff from two local radio stations in preparing the studios and formulating programs to be broadcast from them.

From August 7 to August 12, 1939, two formal shows were performed and broadcast each day from 9:00 a.m. to 11:00 a.m. and 3:00 p.m. to 5:00

p.m. Throughout the week between these formal shows, addresses and or entertainment was provided by Georgia governor E.D. Rivers; Atlanta mayor William B. Hartsfield; *Atlanta Constitution* editor Ralph McGill; singer, songwriter and radio pioneer Art Gillham, aka the "Whispering Pianist"; Rich's fashion models; and other civic leaders and educators. Additionally, golf greats Bobby Jones and Charlie Yates and tennis great Bryan "Bitsy" Grant showcased their sports moves in the studio. Over the six-day period, more than forty thousand visitors crowded into Rich's tearoom to witness the events.

Ironically, television sets were not yet sold at Rich's. At this time, television was not quite perfected, and commercial use was several years away. It was not until shortly after World War II that television sets started appearing in Georgia's households.

Chapter 7

GIVING RICH'S

(1940s)

Despite most of the country still reeling from the economic realities of the Great Depression, which would linger on into the 1940s before World War II would alleviate them, Rich's thrived. Not only did the company's coffers continue to collect money, but the store also continued to heavily expand its physical presence and give to its community.

In September 1940, Rich's completed a $1 million expansion announced a year earlier. Making it the largest department store south of the Mason-Dixon line, the expansion included the installation of escalators connecting the first three floors of the 1924 store to each other, a new warehouse built across Forsyth Street from the main store with two underground tunnels connecting the pair, a large addition to the basement and new shipping rooms at the back of the store. The largest single addition, however, was a five-story wing added to the southern end of the existing store. Designed by Hentz, Adler & Shutze, this wing contained a subbasement, basement, first floor, mezzanine, two completed floors and two partially completed floors. The addition, though modernist in design, was clad in beige brick to match the original 1924 building it adjoined.

Within this five-story addition was Rich's new Store for Men, a department designed with its own "men's" entrance off Broad Street and offering expanded lines of men's clothing. Another new department within the addition was Rich's Store for Homes, which offered consolidated home furnishings. One set of home furnishings offered was its Regency Ensemble line. This line, the only completely coordinated collection of home furnishings in America at the time, consisted of over 1,800 items, from furniture to closet accessories, which were designed to go together and were available in seven different color varieties.

Fourteen months after opening, Rich's new facilities, along with those already existing, would serve as the backdrop for its Diamond Jubilee celebrations. While the company's actual seventy-fifth anniversary date was not until May 28, 1942, the company started celebrating in January and would continue celebrating in some form or fashion throughout the entire year. And although Rich's had always celebrated its anniversaries in grand style, none compared to this year's events.

On January 2, 1942, Rich's invited the public to come to its store for its anniversary kickoff celebration. At 6:00 p.m., the company opened for public viewing twelve display windows, dubbed the twelve Diamond Jubilee Windows, which contained scenes of home furnishings and fashions that contrasted styles of 1942 with those of 1867. Also opened in front of the store on Broad Street was a replica of Morris Rich's 1867 M. Rich & Co. store, replete with relics of the time. At 8:00 p.m., the store officially opened its anniversary festivities inside the sprawling complex.

Taking center stage for the official kickoff event was Margaret Mitchell, author of *Gone with the Wind*, who unveiled five murals painted to commemorate Rich's seventy-five years in business. Mitchell was no stranger to Rich's; she knew Richard Rich personally and had shopped at the store for years. She once was caught half-naked in a Rich's dressing room by a group of women wanting to glimpse Atlanta's newest celebrity days after her novel had been published.[18] Three years later, for the 1939 premiere of the movie based on her book, she purchased off the rack at Rich's an evening jacket to wear for the event.

The murals she unveiled were painted by Witold Gordon, Wilbur Kurtz and John M. Sitton and were located on the street level of Rich's 1924 building, by this time referred to as the Store for Fashion. Gordon, whose two 11.0- by 8.0-foot murals, *Flowers of Georgia* and *Fruits of Georgia*, depicted fashion designs done in colors of Georgia's native flowers and fruits, was a Polish-born New York muralist noted for his murals and posters painted for Radio City Music Hall, the 1932 Olympics and the 1939 New York World's Fair. Kurtz, whose 53.4- by 4.6-foot mural, *Fashion Through the Years*, depicted changes in women's fashions from 1867 to 1942, was a prominent Atlanta painter known for his work on Atlanta's Cyclorama and for being a technical advisor in Hollywood on the movie *Gone with the Wind*. Sitton, whose two 18.0- by 8.0-foot murals, *The Legend of Georgia* and *The Legend of Atlanta*, depicted highlights of Georgia and Atlanta history, was a Georgia painter known for the several murals he painted across the country in Federal Reserve Banks.

After the murals were unveiled, the public heard remarks from guest speakers such as Preston S. Arkwright, president of the Georgia Power Company, and were entertained by Rich's Choral Club and Bill Clarke's orchestra. Also, Atlanta sculptor Julian H. Harris's Rich's Diamond Jubilee Medallion was made available for purchase. The medallion on one side symbolized Atlanta as a phoenix rising from its ashes, clutching the U.S. and Confederate flags. On the reverse side was the star and crescent, a symbol of Rich's, and the words "Friendship, Honor, Service." A six-foot reproduction of the medallion also was displayed on a revolving base in the store, where it would remain throughout the year.

The day after Margaret Mitchell kicked off Rich's Diamond Jubilee celebrations, the company hosted an elaborate luncheon for seventy-five of its most loyal customers in its newly renovated tearoom, the Magnolia Room. Also in attendance at the event were Walter Rich, Frank Neely and many prominent members of Atlanta society, who were entertained by store personnel in a program centering on the company's Diamond Jubilee.

THE MAGNOLIA ROOM

Over the last several months of 1941, Rich's original tearoom, which since 1924 had simply been called the "Tea Room," was redecorated in the Southern Colonial style, rechristened as the Magnolia Room and officially opened in January 1942. Tall white columns marked the entrance to the restaurant just off the store's sixth-floor elevator lobby. The walls were painted magnolia green and table linens were of mimosa yellow, both anniversary colors of the store, while a fireplace and fake windows added to the room's themed decor.[19]

To complete the "southern" ambiance, Rich's had black waitresses costumed in Mammy-styled dresses to serve the restaurant's white-only patrons. "Lunch with us…in a room that whispers of the charm of 1867… revel in the famous Southern dishes, served by bandanad [sic] darkies. Here is the hospitality for which the South is famous," Rich's touted in a January 28, 1942 *Atlanta Constitution* advertisement.[20]

Originally serving lunch between 11:30 a.m. and 3:00 p.m. and offering select afternoon tea times, which by the 1960s were on Saturdays at 4:00 p.m. and during the weekdays by appointment, the Magnolia Room ventured

Rich's, Inc.—Family Controlled (1929–1976)

For decades, the Magnolia Room was the place to enjoy teatime, dine and watch fashion shows. It also was where Martin Luther King Jr. was arrested in 1960 after asking to be served. *Courtesy of the Kenan Research Center at the Atlanta History Center.*

into serving dinner. Women could be seen dressed to the nines with white gloves and fashionable hats, when in vogue, accompanying friends or family at the tearoom tables, enjoying such favorites as chicken salad amandine, cheese straws or Rich's famous coconut cake.

In addition to serving food, the Magnolia Room, like the tearoom it had replaced, became a popular place to have bridge parties, weekly club meetings or college alumni gatherings. Over time, the tearoom became the store's catch-all showplace, hosting everything from art exhibits, lecture presentations, special parties for expectant mothers and marionette shows for children to fashion shows, impromptu or staged, book signings and celebrity autographing parties.

In the late 1950s when Rich's started its suburban expansion, so, too, did the Magnolia Room, with a location opening in Rich's Lenox Square store and then eventually in other locations. And while well known in the Atlanta area by this time, the Magnolia Room was thrust into the national spotlight in 1960 when Martin Luther King Jr. and local-area black college students attempted to stage a sit-in at the downtown location, trying to force Rich's into integrating its dining facilities. With integration occurring a year later, the multiple Magnolia Rooms prospered for several more years until a trend to gradually close some of them had taken over in the 1980s, with Lenox's Magnolia Room closing by 1985.

The original Magnolia Room operated until July 1991, when the downtown Rich's was closed as a result of company restructuring by Rich's then-parent company, Federated Department Stores.

Heading into 1943 with realized sales from the previous year of more than $13.5 million and being a newly minted member of the Associated Merchandising Corporation, which would increase its clout in buying circles, the year would be one marked not by what Rich's had achieved or could obtain but what it could give back to those who had generously filled its coffers. As such, the first contribution to the community that year would be a $25,000 gift for the United Community and War Fund Campaign, a joint campaign honoring 250 of Rich's employees who were serving in the armed forces in World War II.

This gift was not, however, Rich's first attempt to aid war efforts. Over the two years that the United States had been involved in the war, Rich's had been selling war bonds from booths within its store, outfitted Women Accepted for Volunteer Emergency Service (WAVES) personnel as it had been officially licensed to do so by the U.S. Navy and opened a Rich's Military Store in Columbus, Georgia, which served soldiers at Fort Benning, the United States' largest infantry school during the war. Even when the war was over two years later, Rich's sent war bonds to charitable institutions or churches selected by the wives or parents of killed soldiers who had worked at the store.

The second contribution in 1943 to the Atlanta community, and the largest the company would ever give, was the creation of The Rich Foundation. Two years later, that gift would be followed with the creation of Rich's Fashionata, which would be staged to help raise money for needy organizations throughout Atlanta.

THE RICH FOUNDATION

Founded in December 1943, The Rich Foundation was incorporated by Rich's executives Walter Rich, Frank Neely, Ben Gordon, Richard Rich and Oscar Strauss. The foundation was to operate "as a non-profit corporation with the purpose of distributing a share of the profits [from the store] to the Atlanta community in an equitable and efficient way."[21] It screened numerous requests for funds from the store and searched out gifts to give to the community.

Its first large gift was a grant of $350,000 in 1945 to Emory University. Of that gift, $250,000 was used to build the Rich Memorial Building to honor the store's founder, Morris Rich, and his two brothers, Emanuel and Daniel Rich. The building would house the Emory School of Business Administration. The other $100,000, which was paid at a rate of $10,000 per annum over the following ten years, was used to subsidize the business school's teaching salaries. Walter Rich, one of the incorporators, envisioned Emory's business school as one that would compete with the University of Pennsylvania's Wharton School of Commerce and Finance and Harvard University's Graduate School of Business.

The Rich Foundation's first major gift was to Emory University in 1945 to subsidize its business school's teaching salaries and to construct the Rich Memorial Building, shown here in 1967. *Courtesy of Macy's, Inc.*

The Rich Memorial Building was completed in 1947 and occupied in October of that year. The Neoclassic-style building with Greek Revival features, designed by architects Shutze, Armistead and Adler, included a business reference library and reading room, a librarian's office, seven classrooms, thirteen private faculty offices, three administration offices, a twenty-seat graduate student seminar room and two accounting and statistics laboratories.

While there was a small dedication ceremony in 1947, it was not until November 10, 1949, that a larger, public dedication ceremony was held. This dedication ceremony was held in order to unveil a bronze plaque created by renowned Atlanta artist Julian Harris for the building that The Rich Foundation had commissioned and that read: "To the Development of Southern Leadership in the Field of Business, this Building is Dedicated in Memory of Morris, Emanuel and Daniel Rich, Founders of Rich's." The dedication ceremony also conveniently allowed for Emory, as well as Rich's, to tout the fact that just that year, Emory's business school had been officially accredited by the American Association of Collegiate Schools of Business, now the Association to Advance Collegiate Schools. Twenty-nine years later, the building was completely renovated and a new wing added by architects Tippett Taylor Associates. The building, now double its original size, still stands and is part of the Goizueta Business School at Emory University.

For a second large gift, the foundation in 1948 gave an FM radio station, WABE, to the Atlanta and Fulton County school systems for educational purposes.[22] Each classroom within the city and Fulton County was also given a radio receiving set for the instruction of students. Despite these gifts, Rich's was not new in using the radio to reach and educate schoolchildren. The store had successfully operated a Radio School from its premises since 1943 under the direction of Mildred Collins, but in order to "gift" the station to the city, its control was transferred to the foundation. In turn, the foundation created the Rich Radio Education Foundation, which was charged with a two-fold purpose: to continue Rich's educational radio series, previously administered and handled by the store's staff, and to fund experimental techniques using radio as an educational method of instruction.

In the fall of 1948, WABE in its newly constructed studio started broadcasting its 90.1 megacycles with 250 watts from Atlanta's city hall. The station operated five days a week from 9:00 a.m. to 3:00 p.m. and, by year's end, was delivering six program series to seven cities throughout the state. These programs consisted of prerecorded as well as live shows, and before they were broadcast, printed aids for teachers to use for suggesting related

In the mid-1950s, The Rich Foundation gave more than $88,000 to establish and equip the Rich Electronic Computer Center at the Georgia Institute of Technology. *Courtesy of Georgia Tech Archives.*

classroom activities had been sent out to participating schools. Over time, the station moved into doing adult educational programming at night and on weekends. These programs included shows titled "The Man Behind the Music" and "Music and You," which were about classical composers and musical instruments, respectively. Hugely successful, WABE still operates today and is affiliated with National Public Radio (NPR) and Public Radio International (PRI).

Starting in 1949, the foundation would make considerable donations to the Georgia Institute of Technology (Georgia Tech). That year, $15,000 was granted to the school to equip its Department of Industrial Engineering. Between 1954 and 1956, over $88,000 was given to the school to establish and equip the Rich Electronic Computer Center with the latest in computer technology. In 1960, the foundation donated $50,000 with a matching $50,000 promised in the will of the foundation's then-president, Frank Neely, upon his death for the establishment of Georgia Tech's Neely Visiting Professorship Fund.

In May 1950, the foundation continued its practice of large gift giving by donating $100,000 to Georgia Baptist Hospital, which was used to furnish an outpatient ward, the Rich Memorial Outpatient Department. This unit took care of medical and surgical cases, provided hydrotherapy and physical therapy for patients and contained a clinic for the treatment of tumors.

Over the next twenty-six years, donations were continually given as they had been since 1943. Millions of dollars had been given to almost every major college in Atlanta and to institutions as diverse as the United Negro

College Fund, the YMCA, the Boy Scouts and Girl Scouts, the Jewish Education Alliance, state 4-H clubs and almost every single art organization operating within Atlanta, whether they were opera, dance, theater or musical in nature. Even public art, such as the bronze statue *Atlanta from the Ashes*, was commissioned by the foundation for the city.

In 1976, the foundation's association with Rich's, Inc. changed. Following the merger of Rich's into Federated Department Stores that year, the foundation, not a part of the merger agreement, operated as an autonomous institution. In its new, independent role, the foundation continued to use money generated from Rich's registers prior to 1976 to fund noteworthy endeavors.

In 1981, the foundation gave $100,000 to the Emory University School of Medicine to establish a laboratory, The Rich Foundation Cardiovascular-Radiologic Laboratory. In the facility, a team of doctors, led by world-renowned Dr. Andreas Gruentzig and Dr. William J. Casarella, conducted research in balloon angioplasty and radio-nucleotide studies in order to help diagnose and treat cardiovascular disease. Eighteen years later, the foundation gave an initial grant of $200,000 to Emory University professor of neurology Dr. Mahlon R. DeLong to fund a project of his that would help relieve dystonia, a painful neurological muscle-contraction disorder, by using deep brain stimulation. The work DeLong did provided incredible results for victims of the debilitating condition, and the foundation contributed approximately $300,000 more to his work over the next several years.

Most recently, the foundation has given additional funds to Georgia Tech to help support the teaching of business ethics at the school's College of Management and has given funds to refurbish the *Atlanta from the Ashes* statue and parts of Woodruff Park in downtown Atlanta where the statue stands. A substantial gift has also been given to the National Center for Civil and Human Rights that is currently being built between the Georgia Aquarium and World of Coca-Cola near downtown Atlanta's Centennial Olympic Park.

Since its inception, The Rich Foundation has doled out more than 2,600 grants worth more than $55 million. Today, it is the last organization of the once vast Rich's empire to bear the store founder's name.

FASHIONATA

Rich's largest, most lavish and longest-running fashion show, Fashionata, was first held at Atlanta's Municipal Auditorium on February 28, 1945. The performance served as a fundraising event for the Junior League of Atlanta and raised more than $14,000 that went toward various Junior League charities, including children's radio broadcasting programs and germ-killing ultraviolet lights for Egleston Children's Hospital. Five thousand ticket holders at the event watched the presentation of top fashions interlaced with skits and commentary from various individuals, a ballet performance from the Atlanta Civic Opera Company and musical performances by Atlanta's Big Bethel Choir. At the end of the show, chairs and carpets were removed from the venue's main floor so that attendees could dance to the sounds of Les Brown and his Band of Renown, which was in town courtesy of Coca-Cola's Victory Parade of Spotlight Bands series.

After the end of World War II in 1945, Rich's employed renowned public relations specialist, newspaper writer, radio producer and fashion director Frances Bemis as the store's director of special events. It was Rich's hope that she could replicate not only for Fashionata but also for the store as a whole what she had achieved for other businesses across the country. A native of Georgia, Bemis had an impeccable résumé. Before coming to Rich's, she had worked as a fashion promoter and publicist at New York City's Hearn's department store; had done freelance public relations work for the Claire Wolff Agency, including directing shows for the Ford Motor Company; and had been a corporal in the Women's Army Auxiliary Corps (WAAC), where she frequently gave radio announcements and choreographed, directed and produced entertainment for GIs and WAACs.

With Bemis at the helm in 1946, Rich's expanded Fashionata to include five performances in a week as opposed to one and changed the show's venue. Fashionata 1946, which would help raise money for the Young Matrons' Circle for Tallulah Falls School, was held at the 1,876-seat Erlanger Theater. However, before the show's curtain went up, Rich's had to invest large amounts of money to upgrade the theater's electric system in order for it to meet the demands of the heavily lighted Broadway-style show. As had happened the year before, demand for tickets to the performances exceeded supply. Each of the five shows sold out, and many audience members were left standing in the aisles or at the back of the theater vying for a view.

In 1947, Fashionata came into its own and became a sensational show unlike anything Atlanta had seen. For the second year, the Erlanger Theater along with the Young Matrons' Circle for Tallulah Falls School hosted the travel-themed show; however, participating in that year's eight performances were models, actors and technicians flown in from New York, including famed New York theater scenic designer Albert Ostrander. In addition, Rich's flew in fashion magazine editors from across the country and executives from

Sweden's Nordiska Kompaniet department store to witness the $100,000, six-act, twenty-three-scene spectacle. Bemis accomplished what Rich's had hoped for: she had elevated the store through Fashionata onto the country's fashion show stage.

Unfortunately for Rich's, Bemis left the store just a few months after the 1947 Fashionata run and moved to New York. She had taken a job as director of feature events at the department store of Abraham & Strauss. For years thereafter, she would successfully make a name for herself in the department store, public relations and fashion industries. Tragically, however, her life's work would be overshadowed by her brutal murder.[23]

There is scant evidence and only faded memories left to fill in the mystery as to why Fashionata disappeared from the Atlanta scene for nine years. Perhaps the abrupt departure of its creative director, Bemis, and high production costs in 1947, coupled with the fact that Rich's was aggressively expanding its physical presence over those years, contributed to its absence. Whatever the case may have been, Atlantans cheered the show's return in 1957.

Heralded for bringing back Fashionata was Rich's Sol Kent. Kent had grown up in Georgia, majored in English at the University of Chicago and married and worked at Kirven's department store in Columbus, Georgia, before he came to work at Rich's in 1949. He was one of the first male fashion directors in the history of retailing and is credited by many in the industry for creating a fashion renaissance in the South.[24] So sought after was he for his fashion advice that not only did he help dress many an Atlanta socialite and celebrity, but he also helped Coretta Scott King in 1964 pick out clothes to wear to Martin Luther King Jr.'s Nobel Peace Prize acceptance speech in Stockholm, Sweden.

Under Kent's tutelage, Fashionata would blossom into a yearly, themed fashion event held each September. First planned within the pages of his meticulously detailed "Fashionata Bible" and then realized on stage, spectators were treated to seven-act, Broadway-style musical shows commentated on by Kent, while models paraded around in outfits created by some of the most famous designers in the world, including but not limited to Coco Chanel, Bill Blass, Geoffrey Beene, Christian Dior, Karl Lagerfeld, Calvin Klein, Michael Kors and Yves Saint Laurent.

The first Kent-resurrected Fashionata of 1957 was held at Atlanta's Biltmore Hotel. Patrons paying $2.75 for admittance were treated to a show titled "The Four Faces of Eve," which Kent had adapted from the 1957 movie *The Three Faces of Eve*. The fourth "face" was fashion. Over

Rich's, Inc.—Family Controlled (1929–1976)

Rich's fashion extraordinaire Sol Kent in the 1970s intently watching rehearsals for an upcoming Fashionata production, once Atlanta's most lavish runway event. *Courtesy of Macy's, Inc. and Irene Kent.*

subsequent years, themes would range from "The Seven Lively Arts" to "The Life of Shakespeare: All the World's a Stage." Additionally over the years, Fashionata would be held in multiple locations throughout Atlanta, including the Dinkler Plaza Hotel, the Marriott Downtown, the Atlanta Civic Center, Atlanta's Symphony Hall and the Fox Theatre, where the show had its longest run.

While the show's theme changed every year and its location every year or every other year, the actual format of the show remained pretty much the same, the noted exception being that from 1957 to 1970 Fashionata was a luncheon accompanied by a runway show. In 1971, the luncheon was eliminated in favor of a charity matinee show, which eventually morphed into a two-night event. Some of the organizations benefiting from the ticket sales of the later shows were the Alliance Theatre Company/Atlanta Children's Theater, Atlanta's Shepherd Spinal Center, various AIDS charities and the High Museum of Art Exhibition Fund.

Kent's shows, in and of themselves, or the special guests visiting them from time to time, such as designer Bill Blass or perfume guru Fred Hayman, would normally be the cherished memories patrons took away from a particular show. Yet in 1989, patrons got a little more to remember the show by than just its outfits, musical numbers or special guests. Two protestors for the Georgia Chapter of the Fund for Animals rushed into the show at the Fox Theatre shouting "Fur is dead" and tried to erect a banner in front of the stage.[25] Their efforts, however, were foiled by audience members, who apparently did not mind that models were wearing fur on stage that night.

Kent retired from Rich's in 1991, and the last three Fashionatas were directed and staged by Rich's special events director Susan Hancock and vice-president/fashion merchandising director Shelia Gerstein (née Kamensky). Under this duo and at the direction of Rich's, the show was changed. Gone were the elaborately scripted shows of the past exclusively showcasing women's high-end fashions. In their place, non-scripted shows featured not only female models but also male, teenage and child models wearing everyday fashions from random departments throughout Rich's stores.

The last Fashionata was held in 1994 in an air-conditioned tent on a parking lot at Lenox Square mall. More than 1,300 people attended the show, whose proceeds were going to help fund the upcoming 1996 Atlanta Paralympic Games. The games' mascot, Blaze, was on hand to watch that year's fashions being paraded down the catwalk.

Though reasons such as expense, changing taste and running its course were given by Rich's executives for the show's demise, perhaps the real reason for its eventual end was summed up best by Gerstein: "Without Sol Kent, Fashionata was not Fashionata."[26] In the fall of 1995, Rich's replaced Fashionata with Serious Fun, a much less formal and "interactive fashion event."

With World War II officially over and Fashionata just beginning its life as the fashion event in town to attend, Atlantans and executives at Rich's were looking forward to rebuilding their lives in a postwar world, free from the rationing and restrictions placed on them by the government during the war and trying to move past the grief caused by the loss of loved ones and employees alike who had been killed in action. This peaceful transition to getting on with life in Atlanta, however, was short-lived.

Rich's, Inc.—Family Controlled (1929–1976)

On December 7, 1946, Atlantans were left dealing with the horrendous aftermath of the city's Winecoff Hotel fire. Around 3:00 a.m. that morning, 280 guests awoke to what still is America's worst hotel fire when smoke and flames engulfed the fifteen-story structure. Of those, 119 people, including some returning World War II soldiers in town for a night en route to other cities, died either jumping to their deaths, suffocating from smoke or being burned alive in their rooms. As typical in times of need, Rich's immediately offered to help the survivors. Walter Rich and Frank Neely had employees go out and find survivors and their relatives and offer them any clothing they might need, free of charge. The two also provided from Rich's many of the burial clothes for the victims of the fire.

Not a year after Walter helped bury the Winecoff dead, he died at the age of sixty-seven at his home on Argonne Drive after a brief illness. The day following his death, November 4, 1947, Rich's, while in the midst of a $5 million expansion, remained closed to honor its leader's passing. When the company reopened its doors, a new management team was in place.

Frank Neely, who had served for the past ten years as Rich's executive vice-president and secretary, moved upon Walter's death into the presidency of Rich's, becoming the first non–Rich family member to do so. Neely, however, had been a strong leader at Rich's since he joined in 1924 as general manager. And perhaps more than any Rich family member had done, Neely made Rich's the iconic retailing powerhouse of the South that it had become.

A 1904 graduate of the Georgia Institute of Technology with a degree in engineering, Neely had worked at Westinghouse in Pittsburgh, Pennsylvania, before moving back to Atlanta to work in his father-in-law's candy factory, Schlesingers'. After a stint there, he accepted a job as the director of production at the Fulton Bag & Cotton Mills. His ability to step up and streamline production at Schlesingers' and Fulton Bag & Cotton is what caught the attention of Walter Rich and David Strauss, who subsequently recruited him to work at Rich's.

When Neely started at Rich's, he immediately brought in New York designers and lighting experts and had the store relit and restyled to make it more inviting to customers and to bring it more in line with department stores of the North. Over successive years, he instituted a method of inventory and stock control; had the company start acquiring land around it for future expansions; started a system of letting customers make their own adjustments; and, for store employees, initiated quota bonus plans, established a free in-store health clinic, formed a credit union and started employee insurance and pension plans.[27]

Neely's accomplishments outside of his full-time job at Rich's also were equally impressive. At one point or another, he served as the director and then chairman of the Federal Reserve Bank of Atlanta; as director of the Fulton National Bank; and as chairman of the Community Chest program. Additionally, he was instrumental in bringing Bell Aircraft Corporation (now Lockheed Martin) to Georgia and helped get a nuclear research reactor—which was named after him—built at Georgia Tech, as well as helping establish the university's School of Nuclear Engineering. In his spare time, he managed to author a book and, when not living at his apartment in Atlanta's Biltmore Hotel, maintained a three-hundred-acre farm situated next to the Chattahoochee River.

With Frank Neely at the helm, Rich's, as it had done throughout the 1940s and the decades before that, continued to expand or add services for its customers and employees. In 1947, Rich's, celebrating eighty years in operation, began a new tradition, its Eighty-Year-Old Birthday Parties for customers that had turned eighty years old or older the year before the party was held. Over time, the parties grew in popularity such that weeks before the event was to be staged in a given year, customers eighty years old or older bombarded the store with calls confirming reservations and ensuring that the party was, indeed, still scheduled to proceed. Also by 1947, the company provided multiple in-store sports teams that competed with other retailers' teams throughout the city. At Rich's, these teams included basketball; baseball, such as the store's "colored" team, the Rich's Devils; and bowling leagues.

A year later in 1948, Rich's established its Teen Board. After surviving an application process that involved being judged on poise, appearance and the extent to which the applicant was involved in school activities, girls chosen for the board were trained on the store and its policies. Once trained, the girls would be used to model clothes within the store; do fashion assignments for the store, such as give critiques of current collections; and act as ambassadors between the schools they attended and the store. Also this year, Rich's opened an Out-of-Town Service Office located in Rome, Georgia, seventy miles north of Atlanta. At the Rome service office, customers could select items for sale from Rich's out of sample books and use a phone to call in the order to Atlanta, whereupon that order would be filled and delivered from Atlanta to the customer's home in Rome, or surrounding areas, within forty-eight hours.

The largest addition Neely saw at Rich's while he held the title of president, however, was the grand opening of the $5.5 million Store for

Shown here in 1966, Rich's $5.5 million Store for Homes and Crystal Bridge opened in stages from late 1947 to early 1948. Designed by Toombs & Creighton, the building could hold about 170 average-sized three-bedroom homes. *Courtesy of Macy's, Inc.*

Homes on March 29, 1948. Located at the corner of Forsyth and Hunter Streets, the building's construction had started in 1946, with sections of the store being opened at different times. The first floor and plaza level opened in late 1947, the second floor opened the first week of March 1948 and the entire store, all seven floors, opened to the public on the day of its grand opening.

Capable of housing approximately 170 average-sized three-bedroom homes, the building, the largest addition at one time to Rich's, was designed in the Modernist or International style by Atlanta architects Toombs & Creighton. Employing a glass and aluminum curtain wall system over a steel skeleton, the building's Hunter Street and north façades featured an undulating brick treatment, while the Forsyth Street façade consisted of plate-glass windows attached to an aluminum frame.

Capitalizing on the postwar demand for houses, Rich's Store for Homes heralded a new concept of retailing. Shoppers could find in multiple shops under one roof all the things they would need to furnish their homes. And to help them do this was an interior ingeniously designed by Percy Cashmore

Traditional and modern furniture for sale on the fifth floor of Rich's Store for Homes, circa 1948. *Courtesy of the Manuscript, Archives and Rare Book Library, Emory University, Richard H. Rich papers.*

that coordinated and correlated merchandise, which was lit with special lighting effects designed by R.L. Grant Jr. Many of these designs and effects were even copyrighted.

Upon entering the store from its Forsyth Street entrance, customers would pass green marble walls, tan marble floor tiles and brass handrails to the recessed first floor that contained the kitchens department. Moving up to the fifth floor, customers would find table settings on the second floor; fabrics and carpets on the third floor; bedrooms, dining rooms and early American furniture on the fourth floor; and traditional, along with modern, furniture on the fifth floor. The building also contained a plaza level, basement and subbasement with tunnel access to other Rich's buildings, perimeter stock rooms and a television studio and auditorium for demo purposes within the Rich's complex.

Connecting the Store for Homes with the main store, the Store for Fashion, was the Crystal Bridge. The bridge, also designed by Toombs & Creighton in the Modern or International style, was a four-story pedestrian bridge connecting floors two through five of each building that spanned Forsyth Street, allowing for traffic movement below it. Beige in color and made of steel and glass and aluminum panels, the bridge was crowned with an intricate curved support-rail system on its roof to assist with window washing.

Before the Crystal Bridge was constructed, it had actually been a hot button of debate. As an enclosed bridge structure capable of supporting retail space over a public street, an act of Georgia legislature had to be passed to get the bridge built because the state owns air rights over streets. Thus, the bridge actually helped establish state and national zoning precedents for individuals and corporations that wished to build structures spanning public streets.

The bridge would ultimately become famous not for the legislation enacted to get it built but for the spot Rich's would place a Christmas tree, The Great Tree, starting the year the bridge opened, as well as the spot Martin Luther King Jr. would start his participation in the Atlanta civil rights sit-in movement twelve years later.

THE GREAT TREE

Arguably one of the greatest Christmas traditions in Atlanta is the lighting of what started out as Rich's Great Tree but is now known as Macy's Great Tree. Every Thanksgiving evening for more than six decades, hundreds of thousands of people from Atlanta, surrounding cities and towns, bordering states and visitors from abroad have witnessed the annual holiday tradition. It includes not only the lighting of the actual Christmas tree but also musical performances by local choirs and internationally renowned recording artists, reflections on the meaning of the Christmas season and, most recently, a fireworks show. After the tree-lighting ceremony, the tree graces the Atlanta sky until the end of the Christmas season.

Unfortunately, no one quite knows for certain who came up with the original idea in 1948 of placing a large Christmas tree on top of Rich's newly constructed four-story, glass and steel Crystal Bridge. Many people claim the idea was the brainchild of former Rich's executive Joseph Guillozet, who once headed the advertising department. Others claim the tradition might have been a suggestion from one of the store's long-forgotten secretaries. Most, however, believe and give credit to Frank Pallotta, who was the head of Rich's design and display department during the late 1940s. Jimmy Rickerson, head of the poster department for Rich's in the 1960s, stated he recalled Pallotta leaving the store one night, looking

Cars pass beneath Rich's Great Tree atop the Crystal Bridge as trolley buses line the curb along Forsyth Street to pick up passengers, circa early 1950s. *Photo by Kenneth Rogers, courtesy of the Kenan Research Center at the Atlanta History Center.*

up at the bridge spanning the street and exclaiming, "God, what a place for a Christmas tree!"[28]

Pallotta was right; regardless of who actually conceived of the idea, the bridge was the perfect spot to place a tree. On top of the bridge, the tree loomed over five stories above the ground and was easily seen from many different vantage points within the city, including nearby streets and office buildings, and from spots along the highways and roads leading into the city's center.

The actual search for the perfect Christmas tree for Rich's to use would start as early as September. The tree had to be at least sixty feet tall, with a spread of approximately thirty-five feet at its base, and taper upward. Most often, white pines would be used; however, spruces and cedars also were used, with the average age of the trees being between twenty-five and thirty-five years old. After the first Great Tree was erected, Rich's kept a running list of potential trees it could use for future tree-lighting events. Additionally, each year, the store had on standby two or three alternate trees to be used in case the one it had originally chosen could not be bought, had been damaged or actually snapped in half when being moved or placed on the store's roof. While many people had served as Rich's "tree scout" looking for trees all throughout Georgia, North and South Carolina, Tennessee and Kentucky over the years, one person, Rich's employee Travis Guest, did the job for over two decades, earning him the distinction as the store's longest-serving scout.

Once a tree had been selected for the year's event, Rich's would purchase it, have it cut down and transported to the store in the middle of November. When it arrived at the store, crews would lift it into place on the store's rooftop with cranes and then secure it in place with cables. Immediately thereafter, scaffolding would be placed around the tree, and crews would start the decorating process, which could take weeks to complete.

Over the decades, The Great Tree has seen many different decorations and themes. By the mid-1960s, the tree contained four miles of wire; a seven-foot-tall star; 285 ornaments the size of basketballs; 2,500 multicolored lights; and 2,000 five-inch gold ornaments to reflect light. In 1985, the eighty-six-foot-tall tree from Blue Ridge, Georgia, contained thirteen miles of wire; 900 ornaments that were twelve inches in diameter; 600 ornaments that were six inches in diameter; 13,000 lights; 900 non-lighted ornaments; and a seven-foot-wide star on its crown. The last year Rich's name was attached to The Great Tree ceremony in 2004, it took eight workers almost three weeks to string up 1,200 multicolored basketball-size ornaments; 60 two-and-a-half-foot-tall teddy bears; 50 flashing strobe lights; 400 internally lit ornaments; and a seven-foot, six-point star onto the seventy-five-foot-tall, twenty-five-year-old white pine from Snellville, Georgia.

As if decorating the tree was not a big enough challenge each year, Rich's had to ensure that it remained healthy during the Christmas shopping season. On its first day atop the store, the tree was capable of drinking up to ten gallons of water. Each day thereafter, the tree could consume up to five gallons. Besides simply ensuring the tree had water, Rich's also added vitamins to its water supply and employed a thermostat system capable of sending out electrical currents should any snow or ice need to be melted off it on its sojourn atop the store.

By the time Thanksgiving Day arrived each year, the tree was in place and decorated, and that night Rich's would light the tree in spectacular fashion. When the tree-lighting ceremony took place downtown on the Crystal

A nighttime view of The Great Tree as seen looking south down Forsyth Street, circa early 1950s. *Courtesy of the Kenan Research Center at the Atlanta History Center.*

Bridge, businesses surrounding the store would dim their lights, the City of Atlanta would turn off streetlights surrounding the store and Forsyth Street, which ran under the bridge, would be closed down to vehicular traffic so that people could gather on it to witness the unfolding events.

In the early years, the lighting ceremony would be kicked off with the master of ceremonies, Welcome South Brother (WSB) Radio and TV announcer Bob Van Camp, reading the story of the birth of Jesus as told through scriptures. After his reading, the children's choirs, located on the bottom level of the bridge two stories up, would be illuminated, and they would sing a hymn or popular Christmas song selection. After the children's choir had finished singing, each successive level of the bridge would be illuminated, and the choir on that level would perform until all four levels were ablaze and all the choirs had performed.[29] Then, a switch would be flipped and The Great Tree would be lighted to the cheers of the crowd below. In later years, the tree would be lighted during the last few high notes of "O Holy Night," sung either by a lone soloist or with the accompaniment of one or more of the choirs. Under the glow of the tree standing atop the four illuminated levels of the bridge, the choirs along with the gathered onlookers would sing "Silent Night," ushering in what for many was the true start of the Christmas season in Atlanta.

Over the years at the tree-lighting event, local high school and church choirs; the Atlanta Choral Guild; Yaarab Shrine Chanters; tenor soloists Michael O'Neal or Sam Hagan; soprano Indra Thomas; singers Peabo Bryson, Usher, Kenny Rogers; and a multitude of other entertainers and celebrities have entertained crowds ranging from 10,000 to 200,000 in shows lasting from thirty minutes to an hour. In addition to an ever-changing lineup of performers, the actual tree-lighting show has been changed over the years. In 1957, the store had Decatur, Georgia's Llorens Stained Glass Studios—founded in 1920 by artist Joseph V. Llorens Sr., who had served an apprenticeship for the Empire Glass Company in 1906—create stained-glass windows for the annual event.[30] These windows were placed on each level of the bridge at its ends and framed the choirs performing between them. In 1958, the event was televised for the first time by WAGA-TV. Most recently, the tree lighting concludes with a fireworks show.

By its fourteenth year, The Great Tree had become such a popular tradition in the South that it garnered national media attention, appearing on the December 15, 1961 cover of *Time* magazine. Twenty-two years later, part of the tree-lighting event appeared in the 1983 movie *Marvin & Tige*, starring John Cassavetes, Billy Dee Williams and Gibran Brown. The movie was based on the 1977 novel of the same name penned by Atlanta native Frankcina Glass.

In 1989, Rich's executives briefly considered skipping the annual event due to financial difficulties the store was facing after its parent company, Federated Department Stores, Inc., had been acquired in a hostile takeover in 1988 by Canadian Robert Campeau. Fortunately, this did not happen, and in 1989, as it had for the past forty-one years, Rich's Great Tree was seen standing atop its perch on the store's downtown bridge.

In 1990, however, The Great Tree would appear for the last time on the Crystal Bridge. The following summer of 1991, Federated would close Rich's downtown flagship store as part of its efforts to shed debt, restructure and emerge from bankruptcy. Therefore, for the 1991 Christmas season, Rich's had to find a new place to erect the beloved Atlanta tradition.

Initially, Rich's thought about moving the tree to its Lenox Square mall store, but many people protested the idea of the ceremony leaving downtown. As a result, the store worked out a deal with the owners of Underground Atlanta, a unique shopping district built around and on top of old street viaducts, and invested approximately $400,000 into the 1991 event. Part of the $400,000 was for the purchase of the tree and new, clear lights for decorations, which would replace the multicolored lights of years past. Other portions of the money were used to build a special platform on top of a parking deck at Underground Atlanta to support and anchor the tree, for the construction of temporary stages for the choirs and entertainers to perform on during the actual tree-lighting ceremony and for the rental of large projection screens to broadcast the event to the far reaches of the crowd. While the projection screens would become a permanent fixture at each successive tree-lighting event, the clear lights would be replaced with multicolored ones years later.

The Great Tree remained at Underground Atlanta through 1999. Unfortunately, over the nine years the event was held there, attendance had steadily decreased. By that last year, only about ten thousand people showed up for the tree-lighting ceremony, forty thousand fewer than the number who had attended it eight years earlier when it had initially moved there.

For the start of the new millennium, Rich's finally decided to move the tree to its suburban Atlanta Lenox Square location in the fashionable neighborhood of Buckhead with the hopes of increasing attendance. The plan worked, as that year an estimated 75,000 to 110,000 people attended the tree-lighting ceremony at its new location, a place many Atlantans felt was safer and more easily accessible than Underground Atlanta. Moreover, joining those people physically present at Lenox Square was a television audience estimated at 1.5 million viewers.

In 2003, Federated, which had owned Rich's since a 1976 merger, combined Rich's with Macy's, which it had acquired in a 1994 merger, and the fifty-five-year-old Christmas tree and lighting ceremony tradition got a new name, the Rich's-Macy's Great Tree. In its second year as the Rich's-Macy's Great Tree, workers were trying to move a seventy-two-foot white pine off a flatbed truck and onto the Rich's-Macy's store at Lenox Square when it snapped in two. A replacement tree was secured, but not before news of the original tree snapping had made national news and been dubbed the "snap heard around the world."[31]

In early 2005, Federated dropped Rich's from the Rich's-Macy's nameplate. The Radio City Rockettes, country singer Jo Dee Messina and rock band Collective Soul welcomed crowds to the first Macy's Great Tree lighting ceremony, which showcased a tree adorned with newly added red stars, Macy's signature logo. To this day, Macy's continues Atlanta's *Rich* Christmas tradition.

Less than a year after Rich's Store for Homes opened, the company's stockholders made a change to store management in their annual February 1949 meeting. Frank Neely, after serving less than two years as Rich's president, was named chairman of the board, a position not filled since Morris Rich had passed away in 1928. Richard "Dick" Rich was promoted from executive vice-president, a position he ascended to from vice-president in 1948, to president of the corporation, a position he would hold longer than anyone else in Rich's history.

Known affectionately throughout the store as "Mister Dick," Dick was actually born in Atlanta in 1901 as Richard H. Rosenheim. His grandfather, Morris Rich, only had two daughters, one of whom, Rosalind, was Dick's mother, who had married Herman Rosenheim, Dick's father. However, once Dick had graduated from the University of Pennsylvania in 1922 with a bachelor's degree in economics and had decided he wanted to follow in the footsteps of his grandfather and first cousin once removed, Walter Rich, whom he knew affectionately as "Uncle Walter" and who

Richard Rosenheim, later known as Dick Rich, stands with his grandmother and grandfather, Maud and Morris Rich, in front of what is believed to be their home on South Pryor Street, circa 1912. *Courtesy of the Manuscript, Archives and Rare Book Library, Emory University, Richard H. Rich papers.*

had offered up the recommendation, Dick adopted his mother's maiden name with the family's blessings.[32]

As a child, Dick had grown up at the store, working during several school vacations first as a bundle wrapper and then later as a stock boy and salesman. After college, Dick worked for a year in New Jersey for L. Bamberger & Co. and then ran M. Rich & Bros. Co.'s New York office for three months before returning to work permanently in his grandfather's store in 1923. Once in Atlanta, Dick worked numerous jobs at the company over the years, from assistant manager and buyer for the ready-to-wear department to vice-president of the company, until he left the store for a three-year stint in the U.S. Air Force during World War II. After his service in the military, he came back to Atlanta and resumed his position within the hierarchy of the store.

In addition to his duties at Rich's over the years, Dick would raise a family of three—two daughters and a son, who would later work for his father at the store—and would volunteer in various capacities at numerous organizations, such as the Atlanta Advertising Club, the Atlanta Retail Merchants Association and the Atlanta Rapid Transit Authority, which would evolve into MARTA. He also would be the force behind raising $13 million to build what today is known as the Woodruff Arts Center in Atlanta as a memorial to the more than one hundred Atlanta and Georgia patrons of the arts who were killed in a 1962 plane crash in Paris.

However, in 1949 in the first year of his presidency, Dick oversaw an organization that had 3,500 employees welcoming 50,000 people a day into the store. The store had the largest private switchboard in the South, averaging twelve thousand calls a day, and consumed thirteen million kilowatt hours of electricity within a twenty-four-hour period, enough to service a town of 27,000 people at the time. He also saw Rich's open its first parking garage that year, which cost $600,000 to build and held one thousand cars. The garage, a welcome addition for motorists who had difficulty finding parking spots around Rich's complex at this time, was designed by Atlanta's oldest operating architectural firm, Stevens & Wilkinson, which would go on to design most of Rich's stores throughout the remainder of the company's history.

Chapter 8

STORE OF TOMORROW

(1950s)

Coming out of the 1940s with new leadership, expanded services and a bigger-than-ever physical plant, Rich's faced a crisis just five months into the new decade of the 1950s. The thing needed to get the company out of the impending crisis would be television, something that since the end of World War II had come to replace radio as the dominant form of in-home entertainment for thousands of households across Atlanta and the rest of the country. And while it was Rich's that had introduced the South eleven years earlier to the "new science" of television, it was not until now that the company realized its potential as a platform for selling goods.

On May 18, 1950, some 1,500 Atlanta transit workers went on a citywide strike over contract disputes involving pay and pension benefits with their employer, Georgia Power Company. A year earlier, downtown businesses had lost foot traffic and sales as a result of a similar strike by transit workers. This time around, however, Rich's was determined to find a solution to weather the strike and to get people to buy from the store. Thus, Rich's, along with WSB-TV, created a television experiment, *Rich's In Your Home*.

The brainchild of Rich's publicity director, Joseph Guillozet, and WSB-TV personality Elmo Ellis, along with the assistance of the store's design and display department director, Frank Pallotta, and independent television program coordinator, Grady Fraser, who had worked with WSB, *Rich's In Your Home* debuted on May 25. An early infomercial, billed as a "televised catalogue," the show ran at different intervals on different days until settling into a daily three-hour show in the early mornings and afternoons.

To broadcast the show, television cameras had been set up on Rich's Crystal Bridge by WSB-TV, where four stage sets also had been constructed. From these temporary studios, Rich's broadcast fashion shows, interviews, book reviews, merchandise demonstrations and talent searches to television sets across Atlanta. Viewers were asked to call the store and order merchandise featured on the show, which they did in record numbers, often jamming the store's eighty-nine telephone trunks. Once an order was placed, it would be billed to the caller's store credit account and then delivered directly to their home.

An immediate success, the show garnered national news, outlasted the almost six-month-long transit strike and ran for more than a year. In doing so, *Rich's In Your Home* became one of the longest-running shows on television to be broadcast remotely from a department store.

Additionally, the successful use of television by Rich's during the strike and ensuing year helped convince company management to relax its philosophy on only advertising in newspapers; however, newspaper advertising by the company at this time in no way diminished. Still prominently splashed in newsprint were the company's philosophies: "Exchanging, returning, adjusting, at any time for any reason, is Rich's policy and pleasure…for Rich's first concern is your lasting satisfaction and lifelong happiness" and "Rich's, where the customer is always right."[33]

It also was at this time that Rich's ran weekly institutional ads, further enforcing to the community that it had a heart and understood the pressures of the day. One such full-page ad of an empty peach basket implied to Georgia farmers that the company understood their plight when the state's peach crops were ruined by cold weather that year and that the store could wait for them to pay their bills until conditions were better.

A little over a year after the success of *Rich's In Your Home*, Rich's made its first physical expansion of the decade when it opened in the fall of 1951 its new Store for Men. Until 1940, Rich's had offered some men's furnishings but no men's clothes to speak of. And while the store greatly expanded its Store for Men department in 1940, the department store was still almost exclusively geared toward female shoppers. To change this, near the end of construction on the Store for Homes in 1947, company executives held meetings to discuss plans to build a store exclusively for men. Four years later, that store was realized near the corner of Broad and Hunter Streets, adjacent to the company's 1924 flagship building. Unlike previous store expansions, however, the opening of this new store was marred with the death of four men who were killed during construction when a retaining wall supporting a city street fell and killed them.

Rich's Store for Men opened in 1951. Designed by Stevens & Wilkinson, the complex contained many departments catering exclusively to male clientele, including a gun-testing and repair area, a smoke shop and the Cockerel Grill. *Courtesy of Stevens & Wilkinson, Inc.*

The Store for Men, designed by Stevens & Wilkinson in the early International or Modernist style, was six stories in height, consisting of a steel skeletal frame, sheathed with glass curtain walls or brick veneer. Made almost exclusively of aluminum and glass construction, the Broad Street façade featured a marquee that stretched the width of the sidewalk in front of it, as well as a glass soffit that accentuated the "Men's" entrance of the building.

Through the men's entrance, which featured a sloped, illuminated ceiling, marble floors, Vertes Issorie green marble walls, perforated steel balustrades and wood trim, men were greeted to a store all their own. The first floor, with a mezzanine, and the remaining floors, each eleven thousand square feet, were designed by noted New York City interior designer Eleanor LeMaire in a self-selection layout. This meant that special lighting to highlight full lines of stocks and different colors to define different departments aided a man in choosing merchandise for himself rather than being waited on by a sales clerk.

The Broad Street level of the store was considered the men's recreational level, containing shops selling sporting goods, guns, fishing gear, boats and motors. The Cockerel Grill also was located here and was a place for only men to dine until after 2:30 p.m., when it was opened up to female patrons. The rest of the store contained a pet shop; a camera department; a smoke shop; hats; shoes; fine clothing, including Hunt & Winterbotham custom clothing; budget clothing; the South's first Varsity Shop, which catered to young men; accessories; and home furnishings. Also included on the premises were a photography darkroom, a photography projection room and an area for gun testing and repair.

The new Store for Men, headed by Joseph Asher, who had started Rich's Credit Union, was moderately successful; however, men still proved a difficult demographic to market and sell to, not only at Rich's but also at other department stores across the country that had opened similar "stores" during this time period.

With the Store for Men not as successful as had been hoped, Rich's turned back to catering to the demographic it marketed to best: women. In 1952, through the direction of Rich's public relations staff, the company started organizing and hosting its very successful, free-of-charge Spend the Day parties. These parties were attended by women's organizations—such as garden clubs, PTA groups or sororities—from small towns throughout Georgia, Alabama, South Carolina, North Carolina or Tennessee that would travel to Atlanta to "spend a day" at Rich's. Oftentimes, these groups had fundraising parties in their towns of origin to raise money to pay for the expense to travel to Rich's by bus, train or plane. Once at the store, the women in these groups—whose numbers could swell between five and nine hundred at any given event and to twenty thousand in a year's time—were given "VIP" ribbons and shopping bags and allowed to roam the store to shop until they were called to the store's auditorium for a catered box lunch. After lunch, the women were allowed to shop again until around 3:30 or 4:00 p.m., when they were summoned to Rich's Magnolia Room for tea and a fashion show before heading back to their hometowns.

Rich's, too, made sure to cater to its employees in 1952. That year, the company formed its Royalty Club, which gave recognition to top salespeople during the company's annual Anniversary and Harvest Sales. From within the group of top sellers, a "king" and "queen" were crowned and wrapped in royal robes as the climactic events of the two sales. The club itself held monthly Royalty Club coffees and semiannual luncheons.

The employees, grateful for the services and recognitions Rich's gave to them, in turn, gave back to the community through Rich's non-compulsory Community Chest program, which they had done for years. Two years later in 1954, the program changed its name to Rich's Once for All Fund and for decades to come allowed employees through one fund to donate to many different charities, such as those for the mentally disabled, homeless, boys' and girls' clubs and the United Appeal. Within just a little over a decade of the program's name change, Rich's employees had donated over $1 million to charitable causes.

Rich's explosive growth over the 1940s, coupled with its philanthropic endeavors and marketing strategies, had caught the attention of University of Georgia professor Henry Givens Baker, who had spent the previous three years studying the institution before his 1953 book, *Rich's of Atlanta: The Story of a Store Since 1867*, was published. It would be the first book written on the company, its humble beginnings and explosive growth.

The year after Baker's book was published, Rich's would expand to Knoxville, Tennessee, acquiring S.H. George & Sons, and open a new department store in that city in 1955. The following year, the company would inaugurate another long-lived fashion show in Atlanta, The Lovett Show, and open at its downtown Atlanta store a children's monorail, the Snowball Express, which would become legendarily known as the Pink Pig.

RICH'S OF ATLANTA: THE STORY OF A STORE SINCE 1867

In February 1950, Dr. Henry Givens Baker, then professor and chairman of the Division of Marketing of the School of Business Administration of the Atlanta Division of the University of Georgia, met and talked with Rich's president, Dick Rich, about writing a book on the store. In a follow-up letter to Dick dated February 24, Baker reiterated his intent for the book, stating that the conceived four-hundred-page tome would be written not in the popular style of the day but rather as a critical analysis of the store that as a marketing institution had exerted significant influence on the community in which it operated.

In that same letter, Baker told Dick that he was versed in the historical method of research and that his book would be similar to R.M. Hower's 1939 book, *The History of an Advertising Agency*. He made a point, however, to state that his book would be more readable, interesting and broader in scope than Hower's. Predicting that the project would take him two years to complete, Baker asked for permission to proceed, to which Dick officially consented.

Researching part time as he was still teaching classes, Baker started his research for the book by late April or early May 1950. In June, he sent a letter to Rich's public relations director, Dr. Raymond Paty, asking to interview store employees, as well as suggesting that the store hold some type of contest for its employees, such as a trip accompanying buyers on a buying excursion, to spur the creation of character sketches that he could then incorporate into his book. It is not known if the store took him up on his proposed contest, but Baker was given a list of store personnel to interview, as well as a list of living members of the Rich family to reach out to, which included the daughters and son of the store's founding members, Morris, Emanuel and Daniel Rich.

For the next couple of years, Baker continued to research the store, compiling so much information that at one point he asked the store to provide a fireproof safe with a lock on it for document safekeeping. However, before completing research and penning the book, sometime before 1953, Baker moved to Salt Lake City, Utah, where he took a job as the associate professor of marketing for the University of Utah's College of Business. It was in Utah in the spring of 1953 that he completed his book, *Rich's of Atlanta: The Story of a Store Since 1867.*

Published by the Division of Research of the School of Business Administration of the Atlanta Division of the University of Georgia through Foote & Davies, Inc. of Atlanta, the book also ended up being sponsored, in part, by the College of Business of the University of Utah, whose dean was the book's editor. It was the hope of the dean and college that the book would be the first in a series of case studies on successful business firms.

For sale to the general public from Rich's bookstore, Baker's *Rich's of Atlanta* was never a huge seller and has subsequently become rather obscure and difficult to find. Fortunately, copies do exist, and besides Baker's 274 pages of text, the book's 69-page appendices act as a repository of intact documents from the store that would have otherwise been lost to history.

RICH'S KNOXVILLE

In February 1954, Rich's stockholders approved buying control of S.H. George & Sons department store in Knoxville, Tennessee, for $2 million in Rich's stock. Founded in 1904, S.H. George & Sons was a small operation

(1953 sales of roughly $4 million) compared to Rich's (1953 sales of over $55 million), and Rich's executives felt it would make a viable entry point into a new market outside Atlanta. While the actual acquisition occurred on February 12, 1954, S.H. George & Sons continued to operate under its own moniker until it was merged into Rich's, Inc. on December 31, 1954, at which point the store's name was changed to George's-Rich's.

Between the acquisition and before the merger, Rich's had announced plans to close S.H. George & Sons' store in downtown Knoxville and open a new Rich's store between Henley and Locust Streets and Church and Clinch Avenues, four blocks outside of the then-central business district. Construction on the new store, dubbed by Rich's as the "Store of Tomorrow," began in 1954 and involved demolishing familiar Knoxville landmarks, such as the lighthouse service station on the corner of Clinch and Locust Streets and the Kincaid Apartments.

Designed by the Atlanta architectural firm of Stevens & Wilkinson, which would win an American Institute of Architects Award of Merit for the store's design, the $3.5 million buildings covered two city blocks and contained 500,000 square feet of space. The main building consisted of five floors, four

Rich's "Store of Tomorrow" opened in Knoxville in August 1955. The $3.5 million complex was Rich's first store outside Atlanta. *Courtesy of Stevens & Wilkinson, Inc.*

used for the selling of merchandise and one to be used as a service floor. The second building, the four-story Parking Building, contained decks capable of handling 1,500 cars daily, as well as a selling floor and a warehouse that covered two floors. The two buildings were connected by underground tunnels, which were used not only for pedestrian traffic but also to transport packages via conveyor belts from the main store to the parking deck for customer pickup.

The main store's mid-century modern design included a façade of green-glazed tile, flanked on each end by glass panels extending the height of the building, through which greenish-yellow stairs could be seen. The sides of the building were faced with red-glazed brick. Surrounding the building were gardens and parkways open in the evenings for community events. These areas, including the building, were illuminated at night by self-contained reflector lamps on slender posts designed by Broadway and architectural-lighting expert Abe Feder, whose company, Lighting by Feder, was responsible for illuminating the United Nations Building and Rockefeller Center in New York City and the Kennedy Center for Performing Arts in Washington, D.C.

The interior of the store was designed by William Snaith of the legendary industrial design firm Raymond Loewy Corporation of New York City, later Raymond Loewy & William Snaith, Inc. Besides containing traditional departments that sold everything from appliances to clothing, the store also contained a nursery, the 175-seat Laurel Room restaurant, a 72-seat luncheonette snack bar, a beauty salon, a book department complete with a lending library, a travel bureau, an information desk, a health clinic, fur storage, a bake shop and the Photo Reflex photography studios.

The anticipation of the store's debut had become fodder for the press weeks and days before its grand opening. *Business Week* ran a story on the store in its July 23, 1955 issue titled "Finally—Rich's Regionalizes with a New Chain of Stores." As added exposure, Rich's executives Dick Rich, Ben Gordon and Frank Neely graced that issue's cover. A month later, additional press was garnered from the *New York Times*, the *Knoxville News-Sentinel* and Atlanta papers describing the store's inaugural events.

On August 29, 1955, a private transaction between Dick Rich and the eighty-year-old Knoxville businessman and former general manager of the *Knoxville Sentinel* newspaper, Wiley L. Morgan, took place in the store's notions department just prior to the official opening ceremony. Morgan, who had lived in Atlanta as a child, purchased for five cents a white No. 60 spool of thread from Dick Rich. Seventy years earlier, Morgan had purchased the same type of thread for the same amount of money from Rich's founder

Morris Rich when his mother had sent him to the store on an errand. In addition to the white spool of thread, Morgan was given a tiny golden charm in the shape of a spool of thread to commemorate the purchase from Morris and the first sales transaction at the Knoxville store. After the symbolic sale, those in attendance headed outside the store, where five thousand people had gathered to celebrate the opening of Rich's Knoxville.

At 10:00 a.m., Dick Rich and other store executives joined Knoxville mayor George Dempster, Reverend William Pollard (a recently ordained Episcopal priest and head of the Oak Ridge Institute of Nuclear Studies) and others on a stage set up outside the store's Locust Street entrance. After a few opening words from those assembled, Mayor Dempster lifted a tiny blue capsule of Iodine 131—made radioactive and supplied by the Oak Ridge Institute, a division of Abbot Laboratories—and inserted it into a Plexiglas tube located on a table on the stage. Using a Geiger counter to tick off a predetermined count, Dempster and the crowd waited until the power supplied by the radioactivity within the tube built up enough to send a current across the store's opening ribbons, burning them away (severing them) in a puff of white smoke.[34] Following the "atomic age" ribbon-cutting ceremony, the store was opened for business.

Despite the fanciful grand opening and much hullabalooing of Rich's first venture outside of its downtown Atlanta location, the Knoxville store closed shortly after five years of operation. Not, however, before the store made a few last appearances in the press, albeit this time unsolicited ones. Emboldened by the sweeping civil rights sit-in movements spreading across the South in the summer of 1960, students from the historically black Knoxville College and other protestors took a stand, demanding service at the store's whites-only basement lunch counter and its Laurel Room restaurant, as well as picketed in front of the store, denouncing the company's segregation policies. Their efforts, however, were ultimately unsuccessful, and just as other stores in Knoxville were opening their counters to whites as well as blacks, Rich's left town.

On January 28, 1961, Rich's quietly sold the Knoxville store, including fixtures, inventory and accounts receivable, to Miller's, Inc. of Knoxville for approximately $5 million. Officially, Rich's stated the store was closed so that money from its sale could be reinvested into its Atlanta operations, which had started their suburban sprawl. Trade sources, historians and other retail leaders disagreed and claimed that the store left Knoxville quite simply because the venture was an unmitigated failure; Rich's had failed to capture the Knoxville market like it had Atlanta's, and logistically, the company was not ready for out-of-state operations.

Despite Rich's leaving Knoxville over fifty years ago, its award-winning building still stands in the city and is now part of the University of Tennessee Conference Center.

THE LOVETT SHOW

Rich's second-largest and longest continually run annual fashion show was The Lovett Fashion Show. Rich's sponsored the show in conjunction with The Lovett School, a private, coeducational, college-preparatory day school for grades K–12 founded in 1926 and located along the Chattahoochee River in Atlanta's exclusive Buckhead neighborhood. The show, which ran for forty-one years, showcased women's spring fashions by some of the world's top fashion designers, such as Coco Chanel, Christian Lacroix, Karl Lagerfeld, Sonia Rykiel, Valentino and Yves Saint Laurent.

In the fall of 1955, The Lovett School's Mothers Club, now The Lovett Parent Association, teamed up with Rich's director of fashion Sol Kent, also the longtime director of Rich's Fashionata fashion show, to create a show that could be used as a major fundraiser for the school, as well as to promote Rich's and entice attendees at the show to shop at the store. Over the years, the money generated from the shows enabled The Lovett School to purchase playground equipment, computers, science instruments and buses, as well as to fund faculty grants, student drug-awareness programs and other programs the school needed or was sponsoring.

The first show, which charged one dollar in admission, occurred in February 1956 at Atlanta's Cathedral of St. Philip's Hall of Bishops. Shows were held each year at this location until 1962, when they were moved to a small gym on Lovett's campus and then later to the school's Student Activities Center.

From the show's inception until 1991, when he retired, Kent narrated the five-act shows in front of crowds of hundreds to thousands of patrons. Themes varied each year and ranged from "Flight to the Caribbean," "A Glimpse of the Orient" and "Fashion Olympics" to "Girls, Girls, Girls," which centered on theme songs, such as Willie Nelson and Julio Iglesias's "All the Women I've Loved." So instrumental was Kent to the success of the show that in 1984, the school's Mothers Club established the Sol Kent Fine Arts Scholarship Fund in his honor as a way of thanking him for his many years of support. Upon Kent's death in 2001, his family designated the fund as a memorial to which gifts could be directed in his honor, which substantially added to its endowment. The scholarship award continues to be given each year to a student who exhibits exceptional creativity in the arts.[35]

Over the years, certain designers or famous personalities either attended or participated in Lovett's show, such as fashion designer Dana Buchman, professional quarterback Joe Namath and University of Georgia football coach Vince Dooley. Yet perhaps the most famous person to grace the school's fashion stage was Princess Stephanie of Monaco, the daughter of Academy award–winning actress and Princess Grace Kelly and Prince Rainer III. Flown to Atlanta as a guest of Rich's, Princess Stephanie and business partner Alix de la Comble were premiering their swimwear line, Pool Position, for the first time in the United States at Lovett's 1986 show, titled "Fashion Predictions for the Spring," which showcased fashions to be worn for different types of spring weather. After debuting their swimwear line to a crowd of three thousand at The Lovett School, Stephanie and de la Comble were taken to Rich's Town Center at Cobb mall store in suburban northwest Atlanta, where they signed autographs for awaiting crowds. Over the next couple of days, the duo would make appearances at Rich's Atlanta Lenox Square store and Rich's Birmingham, Alabama Riverchase Galleria store before boarding a plane and flying to England for a scheduled appearance at London's famed Harrods department store.

In 1996, Rich's and Lovett held their last joint fashion show, which, incidentally, was not held on the school's campus but rather at Cobb Galleria Centre, a specialty mall and conference center located a short distance away. According to Kim Blass, The Lovett School's current director of strategic communications, the show was discontinued because times had changed and the fashion show "had simply run its course."[36] This sentiment was also echoed by Rich's former vice-president/fashion merchandising director, Shelia Gerstein (née Kamensky), who stated that the show was expensive to produce and that it was simply "not the 'fashion' anymore to do big fashion shows."[37] No doubt another contributing reason to the show's eventual demise was the absence of the creative genius and planning of Rich's Kent over the show's last five years.

THE SNOWBALL EXPRESS / THE PINK PIG

Christmas at Rich's was always a special time for the store, and store management always tried new and creative ways to get kids and their parents into the store during the holiday season. Over the years, Rich's, of course, had

Santa to greet the children, but it also used celebrities, such as Miss Frances and the Ding Dong School and Captain Kangaroo, to entice shoppers to the store in the early 1950s. In 1956, however, the store's toy department executives got a brochure touting a popular new kiddie monorail. Rich's executives, unsure at first if the ride would be profitable enough to cover the expense of installing it, decided to give it a try, purchased it and began the process of hanging it from the ceiling of the store's toy department.[38]

The ride, a three-car monorail capable of transporting twenty-four kids at a time and suspended from a four-hundred-foot-long track, was manufactured by Rocket Express Systems out of Chicago, Illinois. The company's owner, Clinton B. Clark, had developed the ride in the mid- to late 1940s. A former employee of Milwaukee's Boston Store, Clark had gotten the idea for the ride from the Boston Store's president, who had suggested making a train ride that would be elevated above the store's display cases in order to conserve and free up floor and wall space.[39] From the start, Clark's monorail ride proved a successful invention. Throughout the late 1940s and 1950s, several stores across the country installed it along the ceilings of their toy departments, including Philadelphia's Wanamaker's, Chicago's State Street Sears, Minneapolis's Donaldson's and Portland's Meier & Frank.[40] In 1956, Rich's added its name to the list.

On October 13, 1956, Rich's launched its kiddie monorail ride, the Snowball Express, for its inaugural run at 9:30 a.m. The monorail, complete with a single front headlight, three car compartments with four mesh-covered windows each and a rocket-shaped tail, transported children under ten years of age across the ceiling of Rich's toy department for ten cents a ride.[41] The Snowball Express's debut was such a success that within two weeks of its premiere, the ride had garnered national media attention. Universal News visited Rich's Winter Toy Carnival in October of that year and filmed a segment of children riding over the toy department waving at their parents below to be shown before the start of movies across the country. In Atlanta, the newsreel premiered at the Rialto theater downtown on October 28.[42]

After the first season of having the monorail, Rich's executives no longer had to worry about the cost of the ride outweighing the profits they would make from it. Within the first year, Rich's Snowball Express had carried ninety thousand kids, and perhaps a few adults, across the ceiling of its toy department, netting $9,000 in sales.[43]

For the 1957 Christmas season, Rich's decided to rebrand the monorail and named it the Sky Ride. In 1958, the store changed the name of the ride again and called it Rich's Giantland Monorail Express, or the Giant

A view of the Snowball Express during its debut in October 1956. Three years later, the monorail would become the Pink Pig Flyer. *Courtesy of eFootage, llc.*

Express for short. By 1959, however, executives at Rich's wanted to reinvent the monorail. They wanted to find a way to make it more unique, attractive and fun for the children of Atlanta.

According to Jay Salzman, former toy buyer for Rich's in the 1950s and then later one of the store's vice-presidents, he, along with Rich's design and display director, Dudley Pope, merchandising manager Louis Carrol and other Rich's employees, sat around a table and had a brainstorming session to figure out how they could make the ride more appealing and more uniquely Rich's own. During that session, someone mentioned that they had recently seen a "really cute" cartoon character of a pig and offered that up as something the monorail might be remade to resemble. Per Salzman, Pope thought over the idea, decided it was a good one and set about to have the store reshape the monorail into a cute pink pig, complete with snout and curly tail.[44]

For Rich's 1959 Christmas season, the Pink Pig Flyer, which the ride had been dubbed, premiered for the first time across the store's toy department ceiling. In its first year as the newly decorated swine, the Pink Pig Flyer took

Percival the Pink Pig glides past The Great Tree in 1980. *Copyright* Atlanta Journal-Constitution, *courtesy of Georgia State University.*

children through a magical "Toys Alive" journey, which featured fourteen electronically animated scenes from favorite children storybooks, such as the Cow That Jumped Over the Moon; Humpty Dumpty; Little Jack Horner; Little Red Riding Hood; and Peter, Peter Pumpkin Eater. For the next four years, the ride would delight children of all ages.[45]

For some unknown reason, Rich's determined in 1964 that the Pink Pig Flyer had run its course and was no longer needed as a Christmas attraction at the store. That year, it was sold to a Midwest amusement company, and in its place at Christmas, the store offered children a ride on a horse-drawn buggy through Santa's new Christmas Park, which had been set up atop the store's parking deck. Atlantans, however, were not pleased with the new attraction; they had grown to love the Pink Pig Flyer and demanded the store get it back.

After the backlash and public outcry from the previous Christmas season, in 1965, Rich's quietly went and bought back the Pink Pig Flyer from the amusement park it had been sold to. The store also purchased a second

One of the Pink Pig Twins flying above Rich's downtown Atlanta rooftop in 1987. For decades, the monorail delighted children during the holidays. *Copyright* Atlanta Journal-Constitution, *courtesy of Georgia State University.*

monorail from an unknown location and reincarnated it as a pig as well. By Christmas of that year, both monorails, now known as the Pink Pig Twins or Pink Pig Flyers, had been placed on top of the store's roof near The Great Tree, which stood on the Crystal Bridge connecting the Store for Fashion with the Store for Homes over Forsyth Street. From their rooftop perches, the Pink Pig Flyers offered unique views of Atlanta's skyline to their occupants. Additionally, in certain years, the occupants were whisked above a wonderland of oversized gumdrops and candy canes or even live reindeer—truthfully English fallow spotted deer from a farm in Massachusetts—that had been placed on the store's rooftop. It also was after the pigs were installed on the roof that they started to occasionally appear at Easter, carrying children high above an Easter Farm built on top of the store for the holiday.

In the mid-1970s, Rich's would slightly tweak the pigs' images by sponsoring a contest to give them names. By 1976, the two pink monorails premiered at Christmas with new monikers: Priscilla, the one with eyelashes, and Percival, the one without.

Twenty-seven years after the first Pink Pig appeared and twenty-one years after the second one joined it, the duo had entered Atlanta's consciousness and lexicon. As a result, Atlanta native Nita Stubblebine, who performed under the pseudonym Nita Hardy, seized upon the pigs' name recognition and premiered her theater piece, *The Pink Pig*, at a concert in the fall of 1986. Hardy, dressed up to resemble one of the pigs alone on top of the store after all the children had gone home, would look down from her perch on the store's roof and comment on the city's destruction of its old buildings and, as a result, the loss of its history.

Rich's downtown store was permanently closed in 1991. As a result, Priscilla and Percival needed a new home. For a while, Rich's contemplated moving the pigs to its Lenox Square store but decided instead to give them to Egleston Children's Hospital for use in its annual weeklong Festival of Trees held at the Georgia World Congress Center. There, the pigs would remain until 1995, but by that last year, they were no longer operational and were used for display purposes only.

In 1996, Priscilla and Percival were refurbished by Custom Fiberglass Shop in Sugar Hill, Georgia, and in November of that year were placed in the Atlanta History Center's McElreath Hall for public display. They were such a popular exhibit that the center had trouble keeping people off them.

By 2003, Rich's had a new name, Rich's-Macy's, and its store executives decided to relaunch the Pink Pig tradition for Atlantans. The new ride, however, would not be a monorail but rather a train whose chassis was manufactured by renowned ride manufacturer Zamperla and whose body was designed by Entertainment Design Group, the company that at the time was in charge of Rich's-Macy's Great Tree Celebration.[46]

Opening on November 1 and running through December 31, the new Pink Pig welcomed delighted customers for a ride in its specially made white tent, which had been set up on top of a parking garage outside of Rich's-Macy's Lenox Square store. For three dollars, people who had grown up with the old pink pigs, Priscilla and Percival, could now enjoy the train with their kids or by themselves on a 3.5-minute ride past the original Priscilla, through inflatable Christmas trees and enlarged historic Pink Pig photos and memorabilia and past a giant-sized storybook about pigs. The ride's tent also housed a Pig Emporium, which hawked and sold pig-related merchandise, such as T-shirts, pig-shaped ice buckets and photo packages of customers riding on the new train. A portion of the money from the actual ride went to Children's Hospital of Atlanta, while a portion of the money from the photo packages went to the Atlanta History Center.

During its first year as the Pink Pig train, more than 600 people would be in line at one time to get a chance to ride it. The day before Thanksgiving

2003, more than 1,400 people lined up to take a ride on the revamped pig. Also during that first year of the revamped Pink Pig, the original Percival was placed in a window exhibit at the old flagship Rich's, by then the Sam Nunn Atlanta Federal Center, in downtown Atlanta. The exhibit, titled "Rich's: The Store That Married a City," not only contained Percival but also showcased a desk that had belonged to Rich's founder, Morris Rich, old ornaments from Rich's Great Trees, an old cash register, a 1951 Philco television that looped historic Rich's footage on it and a replica of a civil rights–era lunch counter. Eight years later, Percival would be moved to the Atlanta History Center and join Priscilla in storage.

In 2004, the Pink Pig would get its own book. Rich's-Macy's, through Hill Street Press, published *I Rode the Pink Pig: Atlanta's Favorite Christmas Tradition*, with a foreword by Ludlow Porch, a radio humorist, author and stepbrother of fellow humorist and author Lewis Grizzard. The book offered historical photos of the Pink Pig and recollections of it from the past forty-five years, as well as mentions of other Rich's Christmas traditions.

With the removal of Rich's from the Rich's-Macy's nameplate in 2005, the Pink Pig became known simply as Macy's Pink Pig. To this day, people from all over can trek to Macy's Lenox Square location every November through Christmas to partake in Atlanta's *Rich* swine-riding tradition.

In the midst of opening its first branch store, having the Snowball Express fly above Rich's downtown Atlanta store's toy department and providing another fashion show in Atlanta to join Fashionata in tempting women to its store's dress departments, management at Rich's saw a new trend sweeping across the country: "white flight" suburbanization. In order to survive, Rich's management knew that it had to follow its customers into the bedroom communities of Atlanta, where the idyllic 1950s "American Dream" was thought to have resided. So in 1958, the company opened a new service building in downtown Atlanta in order to supply not only the Rich's stores in existence in Atlanta and Knoxville but also the two stores under development or construction in suburban Atlanta.

The new three-story service building with a subbasement, basement and ground floor was designed by Stevens & Wilkinson and was built on the

Rich's, Inc.—Family Controlled (1929–1976)

Rich's first suburban Atlanta department store, Rich's Lenox Square, circa 1960. *Courtesy of Stevens & Wilkinson, Inc.*

west side of the Store for Homes, sitting below the Spring Street viaduct. The building, which would serve as a warehouse and shipping facility, was largely utilitarian in appearance, with the roof doubling as a parking deck capable of holding between four and five hundred cars. Over the next eight years, the parking deck would be closed and the building added on to several times, topping out at six stories and totaling 688,347 square feet, with two miles of conveyors at waist level for the movement of merchandise throughout the facility.

The year after the service center was built, Atlanta's Lenox Square mall opened officially in August 1959 north of downtown Atlanta in Buckhead, a ritzy enclave of expensive homes that at the time was largely free of commercial development. With the mall's opening, Atlantans gained access to their second Rich's department store. Originally 180,000 square feet spread out over three floors, the Lenox location would be added on to multiple times over subsequent decades, including the addition of several more floors.[47] The most dramatic change to the store, however, was done thirteen years after it was built, when one of its entrances was incorporated into the overall conversion of Lenox Square from an open-air shopping plaza to an enclosed mall. With its Magnolia Room, Br'er Fox Room cafeteria and Regency Shops for high fashion, the Lenox Square store quickly became a favorite with Atlanta shoppers.

Crystal chandeliers hang above the Regency Room within Rich's Lenox Square store, circa 1970s. *Courtesy of Macy's, Inc.*

A month after the Lenox Square store opened, Rich's opened a second suburban department store in Belvedere Plaza east of downtown Atlanta in Decatur, Georgia. Rich's had actually had a presence at Belvedere Plaza since 1956, when it had operated a small store devoted almost exclusively to appliances known as Rich's Belvedere Appliance Store. The appliance store was closed with the opening of the newly built department store in September 1959 in front of the original Belvedere shopping center. The new department store, at approximately forty thousand square feet, was less than a quarter in size of the Lenox Square store. As a result, it did not offer all the departments and services that Rich's Lenox Square or downtown Atlanta stores did. Three years later, however, a second floor of forty-five thousand square feet was added, which increased the departments and services the store was able to provide. Twenty-four years after that addition, the store would garner the dubious distinction of being the first suburban Rich's in Atlanta to be closed for underperformance.

After opening these two stores, Rich's management found displeasure in building within other people's planned developments; therefore, the company started or initiated developments of its own with the assistance of its own personal planner, Alvin Ferst, and his staff, as well as the aid of business analysts Hammer, Greene, Siler Associates. Going forward, this group would survey land and study traffic patterns and other pertinent data to determine where Rich's should open stores in the future.

Chapter 9

ONE HUNDRED YEARS BUILDING

(1960s)

The successful openings of two suburban stores in Atlanta in the months just prior to 1960 were quickly overshadowed by events that played out at Rich's in the spring, summer and fall of that year. On February 1, 1960, at a Woolworth's in Greensboro, North Carolina, four black students sat down at the store's segregated lunch counter and asked to be served. The store's refusal to serve the students at the whites-only lunch counter and the subsequent refusal of the students to leave kick-started a movement that quickly found its way to Rich's doors.

KNOXVILLE SIT-INS

Emboldened by the Woolworth's sit-in, black students at Knoxville College in Knoxville, Tennessee, turned their attention to the segregated lunch counters and restaurants in downtown Knoxville, including those of Rich's. The students had initially wanted to start protesting stores in Knoxville with sit-ins in February but were persuaded by Knoxville College president Dr. James Colston to let him try and negotiate with Knoxville mayor John Duncan Sr., his biracial Mayor's Committee and city business leaders to find a way to end segregation at the city's lunch counters. However, by the end of May, negotiations with city business leaders to desegregate their lunch counters had never materialized, and Rich's found itself squarely in the crosshairs of Knoxville's sit-in movement.

Rich's, one of the largest and most prestigious stores in Knoxville at the time, did not plan on upsetting its white clientele by allowing blacks to eat at its whites-only counters and, fearing that sit-ins might find their way to its store, proceeded to build a partition around its whites-only basement lunch counter, with only a narrow entrance allowing admittance to and from it. A little after 11:15 a.m. on June 9, however, that partition failed to prevent black Knoxville College student Robert Booker and white Knoxville College professor of religion and philosophy Merrill Proudfoot, who was also a Presbyterian minister, from walking into the cordoned-off area and sitting down at the counter. Proudfoot was offered service, but Booker was informed he would have to eat at the store's black lunch counter. The two, who were to be joined by three other students who actually showed up but were denied entrance to the lunch counter area, sat on their stools for forty-five minutes before leaving.

After leaving the counter, Booker and Proudfoot were joined on the store's basement selling floor by the three black students who had tried to sit-in with them earlier and two white college students from the University of Tennessee who had come to help them. The seven of them returned to the basement lunch counter but were barred from entering by Rich's security guards, who immediately hung up a sign saying "Luncheonette Closed."

The following day, a black woman and a Jewish woman—under the direction of Booker and Proudfoot, who were afraid they would be immediately recognized and turned away—attempted to obtain service at the same counter. As had happened the previous day, Rich's denied service to the black woman but offered service to the Jewish woman, who, in turn, refused it.

The Knoxville College students and their supporters were determined to make Rich's take notice of their demands. In addition to standing within the basement of the store and verbally protesting in front of the segregated lunch counter, they started a campaign urging the store's customers to send in their coveted charga-plates, which many did—black and white alike. Rich's made no public response to the charga-plates campaign, and to quell the protests in front of its basement lunch counter, the store simply closed it and removed its stools. However, to circumvent this, student protestors and their supporters moved to sit-in at the store's third-floor, posh, whites-only Laurel Room restaurant. On June 23, two black Knoxville College workers attempted to sit-in at the restaurant on their lunch break, but to no avail. Rich's employees simply ignored the two women as they stood at the hostess stand waiting to be seated. Eventually, the women left.

While Rich's had received little attention in the press in regards to the events being carried out within its store, that all changed on June 27. A little after 9:15 a.m., student protestors and those sympathetic to their efforts showed up in front of the store with picket signs. A group of about twenty-five protestors marched in front of each side of the store, carrying signs stating "Rich's White Customers Will Support Equal Treatment," "This Little Pig Had Roast Beef" (held by a white picketer), "This Little Pig Had None" (held by a black picketer) and "We Are Were Rich's 2nd-Class Customers." By mid-afternoon, the picketing had drawn large crowds. Some people within the crowds supported the protestors, while others heckled them, hurled eggs at them or grabbed their signs and broke them in half. Also on hand was WATE-TV, which filmed a piece about the economic boycott by the protestors to be aired that evening. The protest, having succeeded in virtually cutting off any traffic into the store, ended around 5:30 p.m. with no arrests of any of the picketers, at the mayor's request. Ironically, however, at least one white person was arrested, a boy who had thrown water on a young black girl and who had a knife in his possession.

In the days following the picketing outside Rich's, student protestors again tried to sit-in at the Laurel Room restaurant but were denied service. Also at this time, students ramped up their protests at other segregated downtown Knoxville businesses and ultimately called for an outright boycott of them when they started handing out "Stay Away from Downtown" leaflets.

Finally weakened by the economic effect of the protests and boycotts, some downtown businesses agreed to desegregate. On July 12 at 12:30 p.m., Knoxvillians heard on the radio that a special committee, the Good Will Committee, appointed by the mayor and Knoxville Chamber of Commerce, had requested merchants to desegregate and that they had agreed to do so on July 18. However, not every merchant in Knoxville actually agreed to do this, including Rich's.

Rich's Knoxville eating facilities, including its nursery and hair salon, remained segregated until early October 1960, when executives in Atlanta gave the store permission to open its basement lunch counter to both whites and blacks. When the counter did open, it did so without its stools and was a stand-up snack bar. Unfortunately, the bar did not remain desegregated for long. After Martin Luther King Jr.'s arrest on October 19 at Rich's downtown Atlanta Magnolia Room, the company rescinded its decision and segregated the counter once again.

As a result of the store's reversal and its firm policy of not desegregating its Laurel Room restaurant, some Knoxville College students returned to the store to carry out halfhearted sit-in and stand-in attempts over the next few months. Rich's, however, soon escaped the attention of the Knoxville College students and a decision on whether to desegregate its facilities when the store was abruptly closed and the company pulled out of the city on January 29, 1961.

ATLANTA SIT-INS

Like the students at Knoxville College, black students at the Atlanta University Center—composed of Atlanta University, Clark College, the Interdenominational Theological Seminary, Morehouse College, Morris Brown College and Spelman College—were also stirred into action by the bold move of the four North Carolina Agricultural & Technical College students in Greensboro who demanded service at a whites-only lunch counter. As such, the students began to immediately organize a movement, initiated by Morehouse College student Lonnie C. King, to plan sit-ins and boycotts throughout Atlanta in the hope of forcing the city's merchants to end segregation practices within their facilities. At the top of the student's list to target was Rich's, the city's largest and most significant retail institution. If it changed its policies, so, too, the students thought, would the rest of the city's businesses.

Ironically, one of the first sit-ins at Rich's downtown Atlanta store was a "success." It was carried out by a fringe group from the Atlanta University Center under the direction of Dr. Lonnie Cross, chair of Atlanta University's math department, and not by members of the greater movement being formed by King, Morehouse College student Julian Bond and others. The March 5 sit-in involved a handful of students entering Rich's whites-only basement Barbeque Grill around 3:00 p.m. and requesting service. Surprisingly, Rich's served the students but refused to accept payment for the food. White patrons who had been eating in the restaurant quickly left, at which point the store barred others from entering and subsequently rolled carts of dry goods in front of the entrance to block the view of the students eating inside. Once the students had finished their food, they left. The store, acknowledging that the event had occurred, told the press later that the "store had no official facts on the matter" but that it took place near closing time, not at 3:00 p.m., and that it was "so minor it did not create any commotion at all."[48]

Two days later, some of the same students returned to the Barbeque Grill to request service around 2:30 p.m. This time, however, store officials told the students to head next door to the blacks-only Hunter Room, where the food was the same as that at the Barbeque Grill, and they would be happy to serve them. With that refusal, the students simply exited the grill and left the store. Within days of these events, this fringe group had been reined in under the larger movement growing at the Atlanta University Center in order to focus efforts and prevent chaos and division.

At the urging of Atlanta University president Dr. Rufus Clement, students connected to the growing movement, primarily Spelman College student Roslyn Pope, drafted "An Appeal for Human Rights," which was published in local Atlanta papers on March 9 and outlined what the students' grievances were and that they intended to use any legal and nonviolent means necessary to "secure full citizenship rights as members of this great Democracy of ours." Six days later, on March 15, approximately two hundred students spread out across Atlanta targeting lunch counters mainly associated with city and county courthouses, federal buildings and transportation service buildings, as it was believed public access to those places was granted by the Fourteenth Amendment of the U.S. Constitution. In their efforts, the students were led by the movement's newly formed governing body, the Committee on Appeal for Human Rights (COAHR), headed by King, with the assistance of others.[49]

As sit-ins and protests continued throughout the spring, efforts to storm Rich's were not resumed until the end of June; however, by this time, the student movement was handing out "The Student Movement and You" newsletters throughout black neighborhoods in Atlanta, which urged people to close their accounts at Rich's and to send in to the students their coveted charga-plates. "Close out your charge account with segregation; open up your account with freedom," the newsletters proclaimed.

On June 23, sit-ins resumed at Rich's downtown Atlanta store. On that day, several students attempted to obtain service in the store's whites-only The Bridge café, the Barbeque Grill and the Cockerel Grill. Ultimately, the students were denied service, but as they refused to leave, Rich's closed the three locations. On June 27, students returned to the store again, but this time they targeted the store's revered whites-only Magnolia Room restaurant on the sixth floor. With the students that day was Lonnie King. As he and the other students attempted to enter the restaurant, Rich's lined up its black uniformed Magnolia Room waitress staff to try and prevent the students from entering. When the attempts of the waitresses to get the students to leave failed, the police were summoned to break up the group. Of the students there, only King was arrested, whereupon he was taken to Atlanta police chief Herbert T. Jenkins Sr.'s conference room at police headquarters.

Awaiting King there, much to his surprise, was Dick Rich. The store executive proceeded to lecture King on what would happen to him if he and the students came back to Rich's—principally jail, indefinitely—and that he would not desegregate his store via pressure from sit-inners. Dick was afraid that if he opened up his lunch counters and desegregated his facilities, he would lose all his white customers, a risk he was not willing to take. In response to Dick's lecture, King responded that he and other students were not turning back and that Dick had better be prepared to arrest them.

After King was released, he and other students resumed their efforts over the summer, protesting, boycotting, picketing, conducting kneel-ins at churches and, most importantly, planning a massive sit-in to be held at Rich's in October, when many of the students from the Atlanta University Center would be back in town after summer break. King and the other leaders of the student movement hoped to take advantage of the upcoming presidential primary election between Republican Richard Nixon and Democrat John F. Kennedy by staging a very public sit-in to force the candidates to respond to the plight of the students seeking desegregation in Atlanta. To help garner this press, the students recruited Reverend Martin Luther King Jr. (MLK), no relation to Lonnie King, to sit-in with them.

In 1960, Rich's refusal to serve blacks, including Martin Luther King Jr., at its segregated café on the Crystal Bridge helped JFK become the thirty-fifth U.S. president. *Courtesy of Special Collections and Archives, Georgia State University Library.*

126

Rich's, Inc.—Family Controlled (1929–1976)

On the morning of October 19, 1960, less than three weeks before the upcoming presidential election, approximately eighty Atlanta University Center students descended on Rich's, as well as seven other retailers in downtown Atlanta. At Rich's, where most of the students had gathered, picketers marched outside the store while other students attempted to sit-in at predetermined locations throughout the store's complex at varying times. At 10:00 a.m., Lonnie King, MLK, Blondean Orbert-Nelson and Marilyn Pryce (two Spelman College roommates who had been picked days earlier by Lonnie King to join the duo), met on Rich's Crystal Bridge, where The Bridge café was located. They, along with ten other students gathered there, were denied service by Rich's staff. As a result, the quartet took an elevator up to the sixth floor to try to sit-in at the Magnolia Room.

On the sixth floor, just off the elevators and in front of the entrance to the Magnolia Room, MLK approached the maître d' and told him that he and the other black students assembled wanted to enter the restaurant and be served. The maître d' responded that the restaurant did not serve "negroes," to which he added that if the students did not leave, he would have to call the police. Soon thereafter, MLK, Lonnie King, Orbert-Nelson and Pryce were arrested, although not placed in handcuffs, by Atlanta police captain R.E. Little under the recently passed 1960 Georgia anti-trespass law. The four were then escorted out of the store through its front doors to Little's awaiting squad car. Most of the other forty-seven student protestors arrested at Rich's that morning were handcuffed and taken out of back entrances to awaiting paddy wagons out of view of the press that had assembled in front of the store.

Later that day, in front of Judge James E. Webb in an early session of Municipal Court, MLK and the others arraigned with him refused bail, which had been set for each at $500. MLK remarked to the judge that he felt he had done nothing wrong in going peacefully and nonviolently to Rich's and asking to be served and then asked the judge to vacate the charges. Webb refused, and as a result, MLK spent the first night of his life in jail, sharing a cell with students.

On Saturday, October 22, MLK and all the other protestors still sat in jail, proclaiming "Jail, no bail." At Rich's, meanwhile, protesting had reached a fevered pitch, with the KKK joining the fray and marching in opposition to the students. Over at city hall, Atlanta mayor William B. Hartsfield had brokered a deal that day with Atlanta's black leaders to suspend the student protests for thirty days so that he could have serious talks with Atlanta's merchants about desegregating. The deal was only agreed to because

Hartsfield had concocted a lie, telling those gathered that he was acting upon John F. Kennedy's (JFK) personal intervention. The truth was that Hartsfield had only been encouraged earlier to work out a deal with the black leaders by JFK's campaign's civil rights director, Harris Wofford, who was interested in the events unfolding in Atlanta. When news broke of Hartsfield's claim, JFK's campaign was furious but publicly stated they would make an inquiry about the incident and report back as to what they thought should be done, adding that JFK hoped a satisfactory deal could be arranged.

Later that night, Hartsfield ordered the release of all the student protestors in Atlanta's city jails, which were under his jurisdiction, and promised that he would try by Monday to obtain the releases of those being held on state charges, a group that included Lonnie King and MLK. Unfortunately, the only way they could be released was if the state prosecutor or Dick Rich dropped the charges against them. The following day, Dick did just that when he and his lawyer, Morris Abram, drove to Fulton Criminal Court solicitor John I. Kelley's home and informed him that they did not want to prosecute if a solution could be worked out. Therefore, on Monday, October 24, all students held under state charges were released, except MLK.

DeKalb County judge Oscar Mitchell had asked Fulton County officials to keep MLK in jail and to have him transferred to his court the next day to determine if MLK's participation at the Rich's sit-in had violated his suspended sentence from a traffic violation that had occurred five months earlier. In May, MLK and his wife, Coretta, had taken white author and friend Lillian Smith out to dinner and were returning her to Emory University, where she was undergoing treatment for cancer, when they were pulled over by a DeKalb County police officer. The officer, discovering MLK had moved back to Georgia three months earlier but was still driving with an Alabama license, charged him with driving without a proper Georgia license. As a result of the misdemeanor, Mitchell gave MLK a twenty-five-dollar fine and a twelve-month sentence, which he suspended pending MLK not get into any legal trouble. MLK, knowing about his probation, had actually been hesitant to join the students at Rich's the week earlier, but the day before the sit-in attempt commenced, he had been talked into joining the students by Lonnie King.

The following morning, October 25, at Mitchell's request, MLK was transferred to a DeKalb County jail in shackles. Later, he was hauled in front of Mitchell, who revoked his bail and sentenced him to six months hard labor (later changed to four) on a Georgia chain gang to begin immediately. In the middle of that night, he was taken from his jail cell, shackled and driven 230 miles south of Atlanta to a state prison in Reidsville. However, before that had happened, news of his sentence had drawn national attention, leading many to demand that he be released.

The next morning, October 26, less than two weeks before the presidential election, JFK quietly made a 6:30 a.m. phone call to Georgia governor Ernest Vandiver Jr., a supporter of his, and asked if the governor could help get MLK out of prison. JFK thought that by helping MLK get released from prison, he could strengthen his campaign. Unlike Nixon, he was the only candidate who publicly commented on the events surrounding MLK's arrest at Rich's. Vandiver informed JFK that he did not know if he would be able to help, but he would see what he could do.

Later that morning, MLK called his then-pregnant wife from prison. Coretta, in turn, called Harris Wofford, whom she had previously asked to help get her husband out of jail. On the phone, Coretta was frantic and told Wofford that she feared for her husband's life. Wofford, upon hanging up with Coretta, called Sargent Shriver, JFK's brother-in-law, who was with JFK in Chicago that morning, and pleaded with him to have JFK call Coretta. Shriver, once he got JFK away from those on the campaign trail with him, told JFK of Coretta's emotional state and the treatment her husband was receiving in prison. JFK agreed to call Coretta and moments later was on the phone with her, expressing his sympathy for her predicament and stating that if he could help, all she had to do was call him. Coretta, clearing it with Wofford, broke the news of the call from JFK to a reporter, and news quickly spread that JKF had called her, personally, about her husband's situation.

Meanwhile, behind the scenes, Governor Vandiver had met with Robert Russell, the Democratic national committeeman for Georgia, his wife's brother, nephew of Georgia senator Richard Russell and a close political confidant of his, at the governor's mansion in Atlanta. The two of them decided to call George D. Stewart, a close friend of Judge Mitchell, who also happened to be the secretary of the Georgia State Senate, to ask him to call Mitchell and see if he would let MLK out of prison on bond.[50]

By the next morning, on October 27, news had broken that Robert Kennedy, his brother's campaign manager, had called Mitchell at 8:00 a.m. and requested the release of MLK, which Mitchell had already set in motion. Unbeknownst to anyone in the MLK camp or the press, however, was that it was not Kennedy who had actually garnered MLK's release but Mitchell's compliance to Governor Vandiver's request through Stewart. Regardless, the story provided good cover for all those involved and set up a chain of events that actually helped JFK clinch the presidency twelve days later.

Upon MLK's release from prison on a $2,000 bond at 3:46 p.m. on October 27, Martin Luther King Sr. (MLK's father) and others within the older black guard of Atlanta decided to change political sides and vote for JFK, despite being a Catholic, instead of Nixon; MLK, however, remained neutral. The Kennedy campaign, on the other hand, seized the opportunity provided by the events and created a pamphlet, "'No Comment' Nixon Versus a Candidate with a Heart, Senator Kennedy: The Case of Martin Luther King," also known as the "blue bomb." This pamphlet touted JFK's involvement in the events surrounding MLK's incarceration.

On November 6, the Sunday before the presidential election, approximately two million of the pamphlets were distributed to black churches across the country with the hopes that they would spur blacks to the voting booth. They did just that. On November 8, more blacks voted than had four years earlier. As a result, JFK defeated Nixon by an extremely narrow margin—only eighty-four electoral votes.

Despite the fact that MLK's arrest ultimately ushered JFK into the White House, the gain for him did nothing for the Atlanta University Center students back in Atlanta who were waiting for Mayor Hartsfield to work out desegregation plans with the city's merchants. The day after Thanksgiving, Hartsfield had failed to produce an agreement as he had indicated he would do within thirty days, so the students went back to boycotting and picketing Rich's and other retailers. The stores, likewise, went back to having the students arrested. By Christmas, however, the students' efforts were paying off by drastically reducing traffic into downtown stores. Subsequently, this meant reduced sales. As Lonnie King and the students had hoped, hurting a retailer's bottom line was a sure way to get it to take notice.

With the students' efforts continuing into 1961, some blacks who were sympathetic to the students' cause but could not do without their Rich's goods were ordering items via telephone from the store. Rich's, eager to make a sale when in-store sales were being significantly reduced, arranged to have goods delivered in unmarked delivery trucks to these few, yet loyal, black customers. These attempts, however, did little to stave off the inevitable. By March, Dick Rich had relented.

On March 7, 1961, it was announced to the public that a deal had been reached in which the merchants in Atlanta would desegregate. The deal was struck by black attorney A.T. Walden at the request of the old black guard in Atlanta, who wanted to see an end to the students' protests; by white attorney Robert B. Troutman Sr., whose help Walden had sought and who happened to be legal counsel for Rich's; and by Atlanta Chamber of Commerce president Ivan Allen Jr., whom Troutman recruited to talk to the city's merchants. Per the deal, lunch counters would not be integrated until after Atlanta's public schools desegregated in the fall. Until that time, Rich's and the other merchants' lunch counters and facilities would reopen, segregated.

With news of the announcement, many black leaders feared the agreement would not be upheld, and black students who had been protesting were furious, as they thought they had been sold out. It was not until three days later, on March 10, that blacks resigned themselves to what had been proposed. That night at Warren Memorial Methodist Church, approximately two thousand blacks gathered to discuss the recent announcement put forth by the merchants. Angry, they calmed down when MLK, back in town after a trip to Detroit, Michigan, urged them to let it be the white men and not blacks who caused the agreement to fail. Some of those present in the crowd that evening would go on to say it was the most eloquent and moving speech he ever delivered.

On August 30, 1961, at 8:45 a.m., nine black students entered four all-white high schools in Atlanta. Within days of that happening, Atlanta's merchants did as they had promised and began to desegregate their facilities. Over the course of six consecutive days at Rich's Magnolia Room, eight blacks dined during non-peak hours, easing the store into desegregating its facilities. Within weeks of that event, the store had become officially integrated; Lonnie King and the student movement had succeeded.[51]

A little over a month after Martin Luther King Jr.'s arrest, Rich's unveiled two new Christmas attractions that quickly became holiday traditions in Atlanta. On Thanksgiving Day 1960, the company unveiled its Golden Bells of Christmas in a display window in its downtown Atlanta store. Designed by Rich's display department and then fabricated out of Celastic, a pliable plastic, by the Bliss Display Corporation of New York, the display consisted of thirty-six bells that moved by hidden electronics in tandem to taped music. The company also introduced Santa's Secret Shop at this time. At the shop, kids aided by a costumed employee could pick out gifts in "secret" and have them wrapped before being reunited with their parents, who had

A gift to the City of Atlanta in 1960, Rich's Golden Bells of Christmas were replicas of famous bells from across the globe, including Big Ben and the clock bells of St. Mark's in Venice, Italy. *Courtesy of Macy's, Inc.*

waited outside the shop's entrance. The seasonal display and Santa Shop, however, were both largely overlooked by the general public in Atlanta, as its attention was still focused on the ensuing boycotts at Rich's downtown store.

Within months of Rich's pulling out of Knoxville in January 1961, Rich's had a new management structure in place. After an April board of directors' meeting that year, Frank Neely retired as Rich's chairman of the board, whereupon Dick Rich ascended into the role. Filling Dick's position as president of the corporation was Harold Brockey. Brockey had started his retail career at Macy's executive training program in New York and became a nationally recognized expert on home furnishings before he joined Rich's in 1950 as the general merchandise manager of the Store for Homes. Within eleven years, he had worked his way up the company's ladder from director to senior vice-president to executive vice-president to become the second non–Rich family member to be named president of the firm.

Within the first few months of his tenure, Brockey saw Rich's end its policy of segregation and open a new self-parking garage at its downtown location, which the company claimed helped it remain profitable in 1961, offsetting lost sales attributed to boycotting that had occurred earlier in the year. The garage, opened in August 1961, was billed as the only such service available for a downtown store in the United States and the first self-parking garage in Atlanta. Conceptualized by George Devlin, an innovator in parking garage technology whom Rich's had consulted specifically for the project, and officially designed by architects at Stevens & Wilkinson, the six-story structure was capable of holding 750 cars. Upon entering the garage,

Rich's, Inc.—Family Controlled (1929–1976)

Cars exiting the corkscrew ramp of Rich's downtown Atlanta self-parking garage, which was billed as the first such parking structure available for a downtown store in the United States when it opened in 1961. *Courtesy of Macy's, Inc.*

a customer would retrieve a parking ticket from a vending machine and then be routed via electrical circuits to different levels in order to balance the number of cars on any given floor. Despite all its technical glory, adults enjoyed most that the garage allowed them access directly into Rich's Store for Homes without being exposed to inclement weather. Children, on the other hand, liked or loathed the garage for its unique, seemingly narrow corkscrew exit ramp, the first one in the South. As with most things at Rich's downtown Atlanta store, the garage would be added onto multiple times over successive years, eventually having a Rich's Tire Center connected to it.

With the addition of the garage, people thronged to the store. Within its walls on any given day, people could be visiting the store's post office or getting their photos taken at the store's Photo Reflex portrait studio. Women could be getting their hair done at the store's Antoine Beauty Salons or at the store's Budget Beauty Salon in the basement, which, combined, employed fifty-four beauty technicians servicing over four hundred customers a day. Passing the women sitting in these salons or people standing in line at the post office or at the portrait studio might be a throng of schoolchildren touring the massive store before heading off to an ice cream or Coca-Cola party provided free of charge by Rich's at the conclusion of the tour.

To entice even more people to visit the store and, ultimately, spend money, the company hosted numerous events in the early 1960s, such as its weeklong Springlandia fashion events in March, which highlighted spring fashions against a backdrop of fresh flowers located throughout the store, and Rich's Home Shows, showcasing the latest in home fashions. None of these events, however, compared to Rich's over-the-top import shows.

IMPORT SHOWS

While Rich's had held several import shows throughout the years, featuring merchandise from a specific region of the world for sale and usually tied in with special store promotions, none equaled the grandeur of the shows produced in the 1960s through the 1980s. Starting months or a year ahead of the actual import show, Rich's design and display shop would design, plan and create a storewide atmosphere for the celebrations. The department, which employed carpenters, painters, electricians, architects, draftsmen, artists and interior designers, had a warehouse on Marietta Street that was said to resemble a Hollywood prop shop at its disposal to help create the lavish store productions.

One of the first lavish productions in the 1960s was Rich's 1962 Europe at Rich's import show. The show contained a bird market, the Marche aux Oiseaux, that was filled with hundreds of birds flown in from all over the world. The birds were available for purchase. The store also created a special area it called La Piazza, which contained a forty-foot gondola made for the store by Venetian craftsmen, as well as a French sidewalk café and Italian coffeehouse, Caffe Ventinore, which customers could enjoy while shopping.

Perhaps one of the most widely remembered import shows Rich's held was its 1965 Italia Magnifica. For this show, the top floor of the Crystal Bridge, which spanned Forsyth Street, was redesigned to re-create the shops of the Ponte Vecchio over the Arno River in Florence, Italy. More impressive than the mock Ponte Vecchio was Michelangelo's *David*, or Il Gigante, which stood on the store's rooftop. Almost two years prior to the Italia Magnifica event, Rich's had commissioned the Istituto Statale D'Arte's Gipsoteca studio in Florence, Italy, to make what Rich's claimed was the only authentic and complete replica of *David* in the world. It took Gipsoteca eighteen months to complete the twenty-three-foot tall Italian

Michelangelo's *David* perched atop Rich's downtown Atlanta store for the October 1965 Italia Magnifica import show. *Courtesy of the Kenan Research Center at the Atlanta History Center.*

plaster replica. After the Italia Magnifica import show was over, Rich's gave the statue to the art department at Georgia State College, now Georgia State University. Ironically, the college deemed the statue's nudity too obscene and had it moved to a warehouse, where it was crated, stored and forgotten about. Years later, *David* was rediscovered; however, due to the conditions in the warehouse where he had been stored, he was in ruin and beyond repair. The college, therefore, had him carried off and discarded in an Atlanta landfill.

In October 1966, Rich's held another grand import show, Hail! Britannia. As was becoming typical fashion, Rich's went all out for the event. Outside the store, full-size replicas of the Landseer lions found in Trafalgar Square in London greeted customers as they entered the Store for Fashion's front doors. Once inside, customers saw re-created shop fronts of Beauchamp Place in London; people about the store dressed in royal costumes; an authentic Madame Tussaud sculpture of Winston Churchill at his easel, which was on personal loan from Churchill's bodyguard, Sergeant Murray; British armor and regimental uniforms; and an eighteenth-century gallery of English antique oil paintings and fine furniture reproductions. On the store's rooftop, customers could shop within a re-created thirty-seven-building, circa 1580 Tudor-style Elizabethan village inspired by the village of Warwick, England, that contained a sweets shoppe, a potter from Wedgwood, a flower shop and a village smithy complete with Shetland ponies.

Also available inside the store for customers to view was Rich's newly acquired coat of arms. In February of that year, the company, with letters of support from Governor Carl Sanders and Mayor Ivan Allen Jr., sent a request to London's College of Arms for armorial ensigns (a coat of arms) to be made for Rich's. On March 9, J.P. Brooke-Little, bluemantle pursuivant of the College of Arms, sent word via cable that a coat of arms was being

 The Armorial Ensigns of
RICH'S INCORPORATED
of Atlanta in the State of Georgia

College of Arms
London.

J.P. Brooke-Little

Bluemantle Pursuivant of Arms

Rich's coat of arms, devised in 1966 by J.P. Brooke-Little, bluemantle pursuivant of arms for the College of Arms in London.
Courtesy of Macy's, Inc.

devised for the store. Rich's, thrilled with the response from Brooke-Little, touted that this was the first time such arms had been devised for a commercial institution in the United States.

The arms, unveiled at Hail! Britannia upon its opening in October, contained a shield whose alternating blue and gold ordinaries (geometric designs) contained drops of gold on the blue ones, which represented the exchange of currency or commerce, and a charge (large emblem in the middle) of a heart and dogwood blossom that represented Rich's heart, the heart of the community, on a symbolically southern image. The mantling (flowing drapery coming from the helmet) was spattered with small charge emblems and was green, the color of Rich's. Above the helmet and torse (the band holding the mantling to the helmet) were the crest, replete with a chain, representing Rich's ties to the community, and a phoenix, the symbol of Atlanta, holding a dogwood branch in its beak and wearing Rich's heart on its breast. At the bottom of the armorial ensigns, the motto read "Institutio Meridiana 1867," which translated from Latin means "Southern Institution Since 1867."

In 1968, Rich's held yet another import show, Mediterrania. This two-week show in October, touted by Rich's as its third major show to dramatize import merchandise, contained a composite community built on top of the Store for Homes, which suggested the architecture, atmosphere and romance of the Mediterranean. In the middle of the community was an open square, the Piazza del Sole, which was dominated by a bronze reproduction of Gianbologna's famous figure of Neptune in the town of Bologna, Italy. Additionally, two open-air cafés furnished customers with refreshments as they shopped in the community that was stocked full of merchandise from France, Spain, Monte Carlo and other exotic Mediterranean locales.

In 1972, tea was served to Rich's customers in a specially built Rose Pavilion in the store's English Garden planted atop the Store for Homes for that year's It's Britain, Luv, at Rich's import show. After having a cup of tea, customers could wander about the store and see an exhibition on the River Thames, an antique British bike display, an exhibition on Royal Worcester bone china or Wedgwood pottery, golf relics from the Royal and Ancient Golf Club of Saint Andrews, British oil paintings by Robert J. Perham or an animated model of the city of London. The store also held a special tribute to Harold Fielding's stage production of *Gone with the Wind*, which had been produced at London's Drury Lane Theatre.

One of the last great import shows Rich's would hold was its Voilà! La France show held in October and November 1986. The company, which had spent the previous two years planning the show, chose France as its import country in order to tie in events to the rededication of the restored Statue of Liberty in New York Harbor on October 28, 1986. Unlike the previous shows that had all been held at Rich's downtown Atlanta store, Voilà! La France was held at Rich's Lenox Square store in suburban Atlanta and at its Birmingham, Alabama Riverchase Galleria store.

To kick off the import show, gala soirées were held in Atlanta on October 15 and in Birmingham on October 19 and included performances to benefit the Atlanta Symphony and the Birmingham Art Museum. Guests of honor at these $125 per-person parties included French ambassador Emmanuel Jacquin de Margerie of Washington, D.C., Atlanta mayor Andrew Young, Atlanta Symphony Orchestra conductor Robert Shaw and French consul Pierre Boillot of New Orleans.

At each store, an eight-foot gold-leafed Statue of Liberty greeted guests, and behind it were video banks showing famous French landmarks and scenes of French life. Also in both stores, the Rue Des Ateliers, a series of shops reproducing sidewalks in Paris, were created. In these shops, one could buy clothes direct from Paris or furniture direct from the Marche aux Puces in Paris; obtain a souvenir from Galeries LaFayette, the largest department store in France; or buy kids' clothes from the Bonpoint Shop located on the Rue Royale in Paris, which was making its U.S. department store debut during Voilà! La France.

Also during the show's tenure, French exhibits of sculpture, photographs and art were housed at the High Museum of Art's Georgia-Pacific Center and the Woodruff Library of the Atlanta University Center, as well as at Georgia State University and the Nexus Contemporary Arts Center. Rich's even hosted French tennis players in Atlanta to compete at the North Fulton Tennis Center and, along with Delta Airlines, gave away a free trip to France.

The most enduring legacy from the Voilà! La France import show, however, was *Liberté*, a stainless steel pair of wings with a 118-inch wingspan that Rich's commissioned from French artist Christian Renonciat to honor Franco-American friendships. The sculpture was placed in the High Museum of Art as part of its permanent collection.

Rich's acquisition by Robert Campeau in 1988, coupled with subsequent bankruptcy problems, essentially ended the era of the store's over-the-top, lavish import shows.

Rich's, Inc.—Family Controlled (1929–1976)

In 1963, a year after Rich's first grand import show, the company broke the $100 million mark in sales for the first time in its history amid rumors that executives were looking into buying Maison Blanche and its branch stores in New Orleans, Louisiana, as well as Loveman, Joseph & Loeb in Birmingham, Alabama. While none of these buyouts materialized, Rich's did buy that year its first computer, a NCR Model 315. Touted as a modern method of accounting by executives, the computer greatly reduced Rich's accounting department's paper load. Within three years, another computer would be added, bringing the combined value of the two to over $1 million. The same year the second computer was added, the pair were linked to Rich's suburban stores' newly installed compatible sales registers, further assisting accounting efforts within the company.

Also new in 1963 was Rich's third suburban Atlanta store, Rich's Cobb County. The store, which opened in August, was located in Smyrna, Georgia, at the Cobb County Center shopping plaza, later renamed Cobb Center.

A view of Rich's Cobb Center store, which opened in Smyrna, Georgia, in 1963 as the chain's third suburban Atlanta location. *Courtesy of Stevens & Wilkinson, Inc.*

The new store, designed by Stevens & Wilkinson with interiors designed by Raymond Loewy/William Snaith Associates, contained two floors that, together, equaled 120,000 square feet. Originally, the store contained most of the departments offered at Rich's Lenox Square store, including Rich's Drug Department, which had been established in 1945 at Rich's downtown store and offered not only a pharmacist to fill prescriptions but also sold Rich's own brand of drugs and toiletry items. Five years after the Cobb store opened, a Magnolia Buffet restaurant was added, as well as a 45,000-square-foot Budget Store wing to its northern side. Within a few years after that and after the opening of Cumberland Mall nearby, Cobb County Center was converted from an open-air shopping center to an enclosed mall. Forty-one years after originally opening, the store was closed, becoming the third store closed for lack of sales.

Almost two years after the Cobb County store had opened, Rich's opened its fourth suburban location in July 1965, five months after American combat troops first entered Da Nang, escalating the United States' involvement in the Vietnam War. This store, located at North DeKalb Center, later North DeKalb Mall, in Decatur, Georgia, was the first Rich's store to be built attached to an enclosed, air-conditioned mall. This store was also the only store built with two separate buildings from the start. The main building, consisting of 120,000 square feet over two floors and connected to the mall, contained clothing and home furnishings, while the second, smaller 40,000-square-foot building contained the budget departments, appliances, sporting goods and a music center. Rounding out the store were a luncheonette on the first floor and a Magnolia Room restaurant on the second floor. Seventeen years after opening, the location underwent extensive expansions and renovations.

Two months after opening North DeKalb, Rich's opened its fifth branch store, Rich's Greenbriar, in September 1965. Located in the Greenbriar Shopping Center, later Greenbriar Mall, in southwest Atlanta, the three-story, 160,000-square-foot store was connected to an enclosed mall with a clear roof, which gave shoppers the feeling of being outside yet enjoying a climate-controlled space. In addition to regular fashion and home furnishing departments, the store contained a Magnolia Room restaurant and other eating facilities, an auditorium that sat one hundred for local organizations to rent for meeting space and a tire center. Four years after the store opened, an additional 20,000 square feet was added to the facility.

By the time Rich's reached its 100th year of operation in 1967, the organization had become a massive one. The entire company's properties— its downtown store, offices, warehouse, 6,500 enclosed parking spaces and five suburban stores—totaled over 3.2 million square feet, 14 percent more square footage than is available in the 102-story Empire State Building. A total of 9,000 employees—which increased by 1,000 during the holidays—worked within these various properties that contained enough carpet to cover six city blocks; fifty-four escalators moving 650 miles a day; the largest private automatic telephone exchange in the South; and seventeen restaurants, cafeterias and snack bars serving fourteen thousand meals a day. Additionally, a fleet of delivery vehicles by this time traveled over 2 million miles a year, delivering over 1.5 million packages, while an advertising department of 53 copywriters and 12 artists created ads for print, radio, television and billboards to lure the over 400,000 credit account holders and others into the store to rack up sales of approximately $150 million for 1967 alone. What also added to Rich's bottom line that year was the addition of its Rent-a-Car center. From downtown, and later from Lenox Square, a customer could use his Rich's charge card to rent a car from the company with rates starting at $5 a day and $0.05 a mile for a compact car.

In true fashion, however, Rich's did not just usher in 1967 boasting of its success over the last one hundred years; instead, it threw a party, which it had been planning for three years. The centennial celebration would be a yearlong thank-you to the city of Atlanta for patronizing the company over the past one hundred years and making it the southern institution it had become.

To kick off the centennial celebrations, the company first held a party for its employees, the backbone of the organization. On January 22, employees and staff visited the downtown Atlanta store to hear executives talk of the current status of the company and to reminisce of its past. Also greeting the staff were ten centennial cakes shaped like Rich's downtown store complex. These cakes, which fed seven thousand people, consisted of some 330 pounds of sugar and 192 pounds of whole eggs.

The following Tuesday evening, January 24, Rich's kicked off at 7:00 p.m. its "A Gala Centennial Premiere…3 Bright Hours of Pleasure," a salute to the arts, in its downtown store. Greeting customers as they walked into the store were bushels of lilacs flown in from Belgium for the occasion to complement the lavender-blue-mauve décor of the festivities. For the following three hours, customers were free to walk about the store's many buildings to partake in activities including painting, sculpting, music, dance, theater, architecture and photography, provided by the Academy of Children's Theatre, the Wit's End players, Opera Atlanta, The Town Criers, the Roemans, soldiers from the Third U.S. Army, the Atlanta Symphony String Orchestra and the Atlanta Civic Ballet.

The following day, Rich's held an anniversary lunch for Atlanta business, political and civic leaders, thanking them for their continued assistance over the years. In addition to Georgia's governor, Carl Sanders, attending the lunch, Senator Herman Talmadge telephoned Rich's executives at the event from Washington, D.C. Over the phone, Talmadge boasted of how Rich's was a symbol of greatness to Atlanta and to the vitality of the free enterprise system.

Throughout the rest of the year, many famous individuals appeared at the store to debut fashions, such as designers Bill Blass, Herbert Levy, Richard Frontman and milliner Adolfo; to make celebrity guest appearances, such as PGA champion Paul Runyan and Australian amateur golf champion Bruce Devlin; or to read and autograph books, such as author and illustrator Joan Walsh Anglund. Rich's also placed ads about moments in Georgia's history within the *Atlanta Constitution* throughout the year, which it then had bound and printed for presentation to Georgia public schools and libraries at year's end.

Despite all the festivities and guest appearances, what is most remembered for coming out of Rich's centennial celebration year is a book, *Dear Store: An Affectionate Portrait of Rich's*, and a statue, *Atlanta from the Ashes*.

DEAR STORE: AN AFFECTIONATE PORTRAIT OF RICH'S

In 1966, noted Atlanta journalist and author Celestine Sibley was approached by New York publisher Doubleday to write a book on Rich's. Doubleday thought that the store had an interesting history and unique relationship with its customers, which it thought Sibley could capture in a book similar to Emily Kimbrough's 1952 book on Marshall Field's, *Through Charley's Door*, and Margaret Case Harriman's 1958 book on Macy's, *And the Price Is Right: The R.H. Macy Story*.

Accepting the commission, Sibley set out to gather information and conduct interviews, but first she wanted to find out exactly what Rich's customers would want in a book that would commemorate their beloved store. To do this, Sibley met Rich's public relations director, Anne Berg (née Poland), and Rich's book buyer and seller, Faith Brunson, at Atlanta's Oakland Cemetery. On a marble bench in Morris Rich's burial plot, the three ladies conversed while eating a boxed lunch and mapped out what they felt the book should include.

With the direction of her book mapped out and Dick Rich's blessings to write about whatever she chose, Sibley settled down at home, or in a fitting room in Rich's specialty shop downtown that she had been given to use as

The bench at Morris Rich's grave in Oakland Cemetery, where Celestine Sibley mapped out *Dear Store*.

a makeshift office, and commenced writing the book. Upon the completion of each chapter, and unknown to Doubleday, Sibley gave the manuscript to Berg and Dick Rich to edit for accuracy, as well as for narrative comments and suggestions.

Purposely completed by Sibley and published by Doubleday in time for Rich's centennial celebration, the book, *Dear Store: An Affectionate Portrait of Rich's*, hit shelves in January 1967. Two issues were published; one, a special leather-bound gift edition for Atlanta's civic leaders, was handed out as a souvenir of Rich's centennial, and the second, more common edition was for sale to the general public for $3.95. To help launch the book, Sibley held book signings January 25–27 at Rich's downtown store, as well as at the North DeKalb, Lenox, Cobb and Greenbriar suburban locations.

Her fourth book, *Dear Store* was immediately successful. It was, however, a Valentine to the store rather than a true history of it over its one hundred years in existence. Most notably absent from the book was any failure of Rich's, such as the shuttering of its unsuccessful Knoxville store, or any controversy, such as the 1960 sit-ins and picketing and subsequent desegregation of the store.

Replete with anecdotes about the store, "the true church" of the South, the book discussed Rich's legendary services, including its liberal return policies, illustrated by a woman returning a dining room set to the store after owning it for sixteen years, as well as its legendary customer service, illustrated by the store changing Christ's eyes from brown to blue for a customer on a print of Warner Sallman's *Head of Christ*.[52] The book also "extoll[ed] the virtues of baby sisters" in declining to exchange a little boy's sister for a space helmet and discussed the store sending a repairman out to oil a new innerspring mattress that a newly married couple complained squeaked too much.[53]

Additionally, the book was filled with stories about celebrities who visited the store over the years. It poked fun at actress Gloria Swanson standing on her head in a back room of the store after she was a guest at a luncheon given by Dick Rich in her honor and at old Ziegfeld Follies beauty Billie Burke, most known for her role as "Glenda the Good Witch" in the *Wizard of Oz* film, for dragging a bag of jewels worth $100,000 with her while at the store to autograph her book, *Feather on My Nose*. Other celebrities mentioned who had appeared at Rich's through the years were cosmetic stalwarts Elizabeth Arden and Helena Rubenstein; fashion designer Adele Simpson; film star Adolphe Menjou; comedian Bob Hope; novelists Thomas Wolfe, Marjorie Kinnan Rawlings and Harry Lee; writer Richard Halliburton; and Georgia poet Byron Herbert Reece.

Popular from the start, *Dear Store* was republished by Peachtree Publishers in 1990. To this day, the book is still revered by Sibley and Rich's fans alike for its portrayal of a store "that married a city."[54]

It is unfortunate that Sibley did not write a follow-up book to *Dear Store*, titled, perhaps, *Dear Customer*. In it, she could have written about Rich's incredible suburban and multistate expansion, its buyout after Dick Rich's death, its eventual fold into Macy's or something quirkier, such as the woman in the 1970s who came into the downtown store every Thursday and washed her hair in the fourth-floor ladies' room or the 2008 burial of Linda Elizabeth Grubbs Shepherd, age ninety-nine, who was such a loyal customer of Rich's that she was interred with her store credit cards.

Sibley could have also filled the pages of another book with stories of baseball great Hank Aaron; President and First Lady Jimmy and Rosalynn Carter; actress Estell Getty; Academy award–winning actress Dame Elizabeth Taylor; Italian male model Fabio; supermodel Cindy Crawford; Sarah, Duchess of York; pop singers Britney Spears and Jessica Simpson; socialite Ivana Trump; drag impersonator and recording artist RuPaul; fashion designers Michael Kors and Tommy Hilfiger; comedian Steve

Harvey; hip-hop artist and fashion designer Sean "P. Diddy" Combs; and rapper Bow Wow, all of whom were at a Rich's store to promote a cause or hawk merchandise they had endorsed. She also could have written about the fathers of recording artist Gladys Knight, *Atlanta Journal-Constitution* columnist and humorist Lewis Grizzard and Academy award–winning actress Julia Roberts, all of whom worked for Rich's at some point in their lives.

ATLANTA FROM THE ASHES

In 1967, Rich's announced to the public that through its Rich Foundation, a gift in the form of a statue would be given to the City of Atlanta in commemoration of the store's centennial year and the store's close association with the city over those years. It turned to its design and display director, Dudley Pope, to help come up with the statue's design. Pope, in turn, wanted to enlist the artistic skills of his assistant, Jim Seigler, in helping with the conception of the work.

Seigler, a graduate of Ringling School of Art (now Ringling College of Art and Design) and a former set designer for Ringling Brothers, was actually out of work and recuperating from knee surgery at Crawford Long Hospital (now Emory University Hospital Midtown) when Pope paid him a visit and informed him of Rich's plans to create a statue for the city. Pope asked Seigler to "put on his thinking cap" and come up with a conceptual idea for the statue.[55] So while in the hospital, Seigler sketched out an original drawing for the sculpture—a woman holding the mythical phoenix above her head.

Jim Seigler's early 1967 ink wash and tempera sketch of what would become the *Atlanta from the Ashes* sculpture. *Courtesy of Jim Seigler.*

Once Seigler was released from the hospital, he returned to his job at Rich's, and while hobbling around on crutches, he worked out the final sketches of the statue. Upon their completion, the sketches were sent to The Rich Foundation, which picked the one it liked best. Then, Dudley Pope, with assistance from Florenzo Napolitani of the Associated Merchandising Corporation in Florence, Italy, got the sketch to sculptor Gemba Quirino of Pietrasanta, Italy, who in November 1967 agreed to sculpt the statue. A month later, Quirino had shipped a miniature of his planned statue to Rich's in Atlanta. That same month, Rich's had the miniature presented to Atlanta's Civic Design Commission, which approved its design and placement at the intersection of Hunter and Spring Streets between Rich's Store for Homes and Atlanta's post office.

On January 1, 1968, Rich's Frank Neely and Dick Rich presented Atlanta mayor Ivan Allen Jr. with the miniature statue Quirino had sent them and issued a press release to local papers touting the gift Rich's was soon to give the city. Unfortunately, not everyone was excited about the gift, and many Atlantans wrote letters to the store expressing their displeasure that an American had not been chosen to sculpt the statue. Others wrote letters admonishing Rich's for erecting a monument of a semi-nude woman in downtown Atlanta. Despite these complaints, Rich's forged ahead.

Rich's had originally planned to have its sculpture unveiled in the spring of 1968 but was delayed from doing so as a result of the unexpected death of Quirino in January of that year. As a result, the hunt was on for another sculptor to complete the project. Ultimately, and again through the assistance of the Associated Merchandising Corporation in Florence, Feruccia Vezzoni of Vezzoni and Tesconi in Italy was chosen to fabricate the final piece, but not before Seigler and others at Rich's had made changes to Quirino's miniature. When the piece was finally finished and shipped to Atlanta, Rich's decided to honor Quirino's original efforts on the work and listed him as the sculptor, when in fact the final piece was done by Vezzoni.

By January 11, 1969, the sculpture, *Atlanta from the Ashes*, was on its perch at the intersection of Hunter and Spring Streets, essentially a glorified traffic island. The $45,000, twenty-two-foot-tall bronze statue, which faced the State Capitol farther down Hunter Street, presented a woman holding the mythical phoenix, an official symbol of Atlanta, above her head, symbolizing the city's rebirth after its destruction by Sherman's torch during the American Civil War. It is from this vantage point that the statue stood for twenty-six years, ultimately seeing Hunter Street renamed Martin Luther King Jr. Boulevard and the shuttering of Rich's downtown store.

In late 1994/early 1995 in preparation for the upcoming 1996 Olympics to be held in Atlanta, Rich's, along with the City of Atlanta and the Corporation for Olympic Development in Atlanta (CODA), decided to relocate the statue to a more visible spot, Woodruff Park on Peachtree Street in the heart of downtown Atlanta. As its first project, CODA, with funds from the Woodruff Foundation, was completing a $5 million renovation of the park in late 1995, and *Atlanta from the Ashes* would become one of its new focal points. With this planned, the statue was taken from its perch on Martin Luther King Jr. Boulevard in the spring of 1995 and shipped to City Hall East (formerly Sears's southeast distribution center) on Ponce de Leon Avenue for renovation. The renovation of the twenty-six-year-old bronze, which included a high-powered pressure bath, new patina, two protective coats of wax and interior structural repair, was carried out by Atlanta-based MER Art Conservation.

On October 26, 1995, Atlanta mayor Bill Campbell and former Atlanta mayors Ivan Allen, Sam Massell and Maynard Jackson, along with two

A view of the twenty-two-foot-tall bronze *Atlanta from the Ashes*, which is located in downtown Atlanta's Woodruff Park.

hundred other officials, unveiled *Atlanta from the Ashes* standing on its new base at the southern end of Woodruff Park. For the first time in its history, the statue was viewable from a pedestrian level. Before its move, it could only be seen standing across the street from it or by passing it in a moving car.

Since its move to Woodruff Park, the statue's maintenance has been taken over by the Atlanta Public Arts Legacy Fund (APAL), which regularly cleans and waxes it and initiates repairs for it. APAL's efforts, with financial support from The Rich Foundation, ensure that future generations will be able to enjoy what has become one of Atlanta's enduring symbols.

Two years after Rich's started its centennial year of operation, the company was in the midst of further expansions. One of these expansions involved a single-story addition at the corner of Forsyth and Alabama Streets on the former site of the old *Atlanta Constitution* newspaper building. On top of the one-story addition, which only stuck a few feet above street level, was a small park, replete with a playhouse and a mural on an abutting wall painted by artist Vincejia Blount as part of Atlanta's Urban Wall campaign. The largest single expansion, however, was the construction of Rich's sixth suburban Atlanta store.

Rich's South DeKalb store opened in August 1969 as one of the anchors of South DeKalb Mall before the entire complex was completed and opened in 1970. Located at Interstate 20 and Candler Road near Interstate 285 in Decatur, Georgia, the store consisted of three floors totaling 180,000 square feet. The store would also have a separate outbuilding containing a Rich's Tire Center.

Preceding the opening of the South DeKalb store by six months, however, was a new retailing concept from Rich's—Rich's Bake Shops—that by decade's end would become wildly more successful than anticipated.

RICH'S BAKE SHOPS

Rich's had had a bakery at its downtown store since 1945, but its stand-alone bakeries came twenty-four years later as a result of the efforts of one man—Carl Dendy—to revolutionize the store's bakery operations.

Dendy, a seventeen-year employee of Southern Bakeries with degrees in accounting and law, came to Rich's in 1966 not as a baker, because he was not one, but as a general manager of its bakery division, which then consisted of an operation to supply the Rich's downtown and suburban stores' restaurants with baked goods. While he had officially been recruited by Rich's president Harold Brockey to streamline and increase the division's operations, it was Rich's chairman Dick Rich who took him aside and told him that his ultimate purpose at the store was keeping people happy. Dick explained to Dendy that people came to Rich's to buy children's shoes, clothing and furniture and under no circumstances did he want any of them upset because there had been a problem with a cake.

While Dendy had mentioned Rich's branching out and opening up free-standing bakeries when he was hired, Brockey and store management declined but stated that if he could increase profits by 20 percent, they would consider giving them a try. Dendy, with this in mind, set about at the store to increase production, thereby increasing sales. One of his first tasks in doing this was to speed up the making of one of the store's biggest sellers, its famous coconut cake.

For years, Rich's resident baker and the creator of its legendary coconut cake, Milton D. Brooks—known as "Jeff" to those he worked with, a childhood moniker referencing the disparity between Brooks and a brother with the likes of the popular comic Mutt and Jeff—insisted on baking fresh coconut cakes daily as opposed to baking them and freezing them for later sale. The problem with Brooks's plan was that he could not keep up with the demand for the cakes by the public, and Rich's was losing money as a result. Dendy knew that the only way to increase sales and expand Rich's bakery operations was to push toward freezing goods so that the store would have a ready supply of cakes to meet demand. He also knew he would have to convince Brooks of this in order to move forward.

To convince Brooks, Dendy devised a simple taste test. He had Brooks, plus other selected reviewers, sample two pieces of coconut cake, one fresh and the other, premade, frozen and thawed. None of the reviewers or Brooks could tell the difference between the two. Brooks, incensed, immediately turned in his resignation but never made good on the offer and stayed on to witness Rich's bakery divisions' profits rise. The decision to switch to premade, frozen products, not just the store's coconut cake, had paid off.

Pleased with the turnaround Dendy had made with the store's bakery division—and increasing profits by 20 percent—Rich's management decided to open a couple of stand-alone bakeries on a test basis. The first

Shown here is one of nineteen stand-alone Rich's Bake Shops that were located throughout suburban Atlanta. *Courtesy of Macy's, Inc.*

Rich's Bake Shop opened on February 7, 1969, in suburban Atlanta at Sandy Springs Shopping Plaza on Roswell Road. Its décor of pink, green and white accessories, splash-print tablecloths and large display cases welcomed patrons to choose from not only Rich's coconut cakes but also brownies, birthday or other decorated cakes, chocolate chess pie, cheese straws, pecan pie, German chocolate cake and other baked goods. An immediate success, a second store opened just a little over two months later on April 21, 1969, in the Atlanta suburb of Forest Park at Clayton Plaza. By the end of the year, there were six free-standing bake shops. A decade later, the number had mushroomed to nineteen, spread throughout Atlanta's bedroom communities.

All of these stores, which were open from 9:00 a.m. to 6:00 p.m., were supplied with goods from Rich's central bakery at its downtown Atlanta store; no baking was done on-site at any of the stand-alone stores. Eventually, five delivery trucks were used to make two trips daily to each store to keep them stocked with fresh supplies. By the end of the 1970s, some of the bake shops were even offering sandwiches as an added menu item for sale.

Rich's, Inc.—Family Controlled (1929–1976)

Customers selecting goods from a Rich's Bake Shop display case, stocked on the left with plenty of Rich's famous coconut cakes, circa 1969. *Courtesy of Macy's, Inc.*

In a little over a decade, Dendy, with the help of others, had expanded Rich's bakery division ten-fold. In addition to the nineteen bake shops, Rich's downtown bakery was making goods for its suburban department stores and its Richway chain, which had opened in 1970. However, Rich's bakery operations were not to last.

After Rich's friendly merger with Federated Department Stores in 1976, the parent company, Federated, felt that Rich's was a "fashion" store and eventually moved to weed it of all its non-fashion services. The bake shops, which operated up until the end of 1982, were closed. In early 1983, Dendy was relieved of his duties and put in charge of closing all the free-standing shops he had opened, securing landlord lease closures, real estate deals and the selling off of equipment and store fixtures.

While the coconut cake would still be made for sale at Rich's restaurants and within its department stores, Dendy would not be the driving force behind making them; in 1983, he went to work for Flowers Bakery based in Thomasville, Georgia, and retired from there fourteen years later. Brooks, too, by this time was no longer making his famous cake; he had retired in the late 1970s. However, his cake lives on, its recipe still sought after to this day.

Chapter 10

RICH'S WAY

(1970s)

While the previous decade started out as a tumultuous one for Rich's, involving sit-ins, picketing and the closure of the company's unsuccessful Knoxville store, by the end of the 1960s, the company had rebounded and completed ten years of expansive and aggressive growth, opening a massive parking garage at its downtown Atlanta store, adding four new suburban stores and opening six stand-alone bake shops. On the heels of that growth, at the start of 1970, Rich's showed no signs of slowing its expansion efforts or venturing into new retailing concepts. Within three months of the new decade, Rich's had opened two new stores in its newly formed discount chain store division, Richway.

RICHWAY

We don't look like a discount store, but our price tags give us away!
—store slogan

In the late 1950s through the mid-1960s, discount department stores, such as Ames and Target, started to appear on the U.S. retailing scene. These stores, offering a variety of merchandise from clothing to electronics and appliances, operated on a high-volume, low-profit-margin business model. Architecturally simple, they were laid out in a self-service format and offered limited customer service, shopping carts and centralized check-outs, which kept operating costs low. Their success, bolstered by increasingly cost-conscious customers, began to encroach on department store revenues. As a result, department stores across the country, such as Rich's, began to search for ways to compete with these new competitors.

By the late 1960s, Rich's had decided to enter into the discount retailer market and in 1968 explored an arrangement with the Dayton Corporation as co-owners on a joint venture to open Target stores in the South, to be known as Target Store South. This arrangement, however, never materialized past planning stages, as Rich's decided to navigate the discount retailing scene on its own.

On May 28, 1969, at a Rich's annual stockholders meeting, Dick Rich announced that the company would be opening its own autonomous discount store, ARCO (an acronym for A Rich's Company), in 1970. It was Rich's intent for these stores to directly compete with Kmart, Zayre, Gibson and JCPenney's Treasure Island and other discount department stores in Atlanta and throughout the South.

When Rich's announced its plans to the public that year of its intent to enter the discount retailing field, many of its longtime customers were less than excited. Scores of letters were sent to store management expressing the belief that the new discount chain would cheapen and sully the reputation Rich's had built for itself over the years as a prominent department store. Undeterred, the company corresponded back to these customers, allaying their fears and maintaining that Rich's would still be Rich's.

Less than a year later, on March 2, 1970, Rich's opened the first two of its autonomous discount stores simultaneously under the name Richway, as opposed to the previously decided, awkward ARCO banner. The suburban Atlanta stores—one on Covington Highway in DeKalb County and the other on Cobb Parkway in Cobb County—were 160,000 square feet in size.

Designed by Rich's stalwart, go-to Atlanta architectural firm Stevens & Wilkinson, the exterior of the stores, clad in gold-colored brick with an upper portion finished in white stucco, contained large glass entrances and eight distinctive, wedge-shaped skylights. The interiors of the stores, designed by Rich's store planning division with the assistance of Jerry Miller of New York City acting as an interior design consultant, contained departments differentiated from each other by different wall color treatments and distinctive floor designs.

Under the direction of Alan Ferguson, senior vice-president of merchandising and publicity, and John Weitnauer, senior vice-president of stores and operations, the stores not only offered customers the chance

Originally intended to be named ARCO, Rich's Richway discount stores premiered in March 1970 with two locations and within a decade had grown to over twenty, including this Decker Boulevard location in Columbia, South Carolina. *Courtesy of Stevens & Wilkinson, Inc.*

to buy national and Richway-labeled brands of clothing, decorative home furnishings, housewares, toys, garden supplies, appliances, sporting goods and automotive supplies with their Richway credit cards or other methods but also the chance to buy from its in-store bakeries, the Strawberry Room snack bars and twenty-seven-thousand-square-foot grocery stores. Additionally, in a separate building in front of the main store, customers could buy Richway brand gasoline or have their cars serviced in a Richway automotive center, which did everything from changing tires to engine repair.

Immediately successful, Richway expanded to include four stores within its first year of operation, adding two locations south of Atlanta. In 1972, a fifth store was added, and a year later, the store's first location outside of Georgia in Charlotte, North Carolina, was opened. Exponential growth continued throughout the 1970s, with the chain opening ten stores by 1976; fifteen stores by 1977, including an entry into Columbia, South Carolina; seventeen stores by 1978; and twenty-one stores by the end of the decade, with sales totaling over $200 million in 1979.

In early 1980, Rich's parent company, Federated Department Stores, which acquired Rich's in a 1976 merger, removed Richway from Rich's control and

A view of a Richway's twenty-seven-thousand-square-foot grocery, circa 1970. *Courtesy of the Manuscript, Archives and Rare Book Library, Emory University, Richard H. Rich papers.*

"The Fling" department inside a Richway, circa 1970. *Courtesy of the Manuscript, Archives and Rare Book Library, Emory University, Richard H. Rich papers.*

made the chain a separate division under the Federated umbrella. A year later in 1981, Richway moved into its fourth market in Tennessee and by 1982 had moved into its fifth market, south Florida, where it absorbed some of Federated's Gold Triangle stores that had been shuttered the previous year. By 1984, the chain operated thirty-one stores with sales well above $300 million.

In 1986, Federated consolidated Richway with its forty-five-store Gold Circle chain into a single division to be headquartered out of Columbus, Ohio, with each retaining its separate name. Combined, the new division, containing seventy-six stores, operated in eight states, the five Richway had a presence in plus three others: Kentucky, New York and Ohio. This new alliance, however, was short-lived.

In mid-1988, Canadian Robert Campeau assumed the reins of Federated in a hostile takeover and quickly moved to liquidate Richway, Gold Circle and other Federated divisions to help pay for debts incurred by the acquisition. On September 7, 1988, thirty-one Richway and Gold Circle stores were sold to Target Stores, then a division of Dayton Hudson Corp., giving them an entrance into the Southeast and, ironically, bringing their connection with Rich's full circle.

Even though Richway was around for a relatively short time, it did prove to be the training ground for many people's retailing careers including, most notably perhaps, Walmart's current CEO, Michael Duke, who started at the store after graduating from Georgia Tech. Perhaps some of the lessons learned and philosophies gleaned from Richway continue on through Duke at Walmart. For those wanting a more tangible connection, one of the first two Richways ever opened operates to this day as a Target on Cobb Parkway in Smyrna, Georgia.

With its new Richway chain open and successfully generating increased sales revenue for the entire company, Rich's reached for the first time in its history sales of over $200 million in 1970. Also contributing to those increased sales revenues that year were Rich's aggressive television ads enticing customers into its stores by promising easy credit, no-hassle returns, the latest in fashion trends, shopping excitement, low prices and friendly store personnel. These ads not only brought customers into the stores but also won numerous industry accolades, including a first-place Phoenix Award issued by the Atlanta Ad Club, a first-place American Advertising Federation in the Deep South award and a silver award, the year before, at the International Film TV Festival in New York City.

By 1970, Rich's downtown service facility had grown too small to service the growing company's multiple stores and endeavors. Therefore, in early 1971, Rich's moved most of the services offered in its downtown service center to a new facility located off Stone Mountain Freeway, a limited-access highway connecting Interstate 285 east of Atlanta to the suburbs of Stone Mountain and Snellville. The new 743,000-square-foot Rich's Service Center offered space for the company's television and appliance repair departments; drapery, rug and furniture upholstery departments; and an employee cafeteria, kitchen, nursing clinic and recreation room for its seven hundred employees. The largest part of the new facility, however, was the 566,000 square feet of space that would be used for receiving merchandise and storing goods. With part of the facility built directly over railroad tracks, twelve train cars at a time could be unloaded while sheltered from the weather outside. Tractor trailers also could be unloaded at the center's thirteen covered loading docks. Once the train cars or trucks were unloaded, 570 tow-line carts electronically routed on 1.3 miles of semiautomatic tow lines delivered merchandise to its appropriate location within the warehouse, and unloading these carts were self-steering order pickers placing bulk merchandise on 30-foot-high storage shelves. Also within the 566,000-square-foot receiving and storage space was Rich's Delivery operations, which consisted of 209 vehicles. These vehicles were maintained by a fleet maintenance crew that not only ensured that the vehicles were kept mechanically sound but also gassed up, using the center's on-site fueling station. Of these 209, 55 were radio-equipped and routed across the city using the center's radio control station.

Seven years after the center opened, most of the merchandising operations that had remained downtown were finally moved to the Stone Mountain location. It was also at this time that the center underwent yet another expansion, increasing the center to 955,000 square feet, or about the size of five suburban Rich's stores or ten football fields or seventeen acres. Over the next several decades, the center would double in size, and once Federated Department Stores had acquired both Rich's and Macy's, it would serve as a distribution center for both chains before their eventual mergers in 2003.

In May 1971, a few months after the new Service Center opened, Rich's added a forty-thousand-square-foot Discount Home Store to it. This new store, complete with 120 fully furnished display rooms, offered special lines of furniture, televisions, appliances and carpets to the public at discount prices. Also unique at the time was that the store offered merchandise for sale that was still housed in its original shipping cartons. If a customer chose to purchase and take the merchandise home with them in the carton rather than having it delivered and installed by Rich's employees, they would be offered a "Take With" price, which was less than the already discounted price marked on the merchandise.

Three months after the Discount Home Store opened, Rich's opened its seventh suburban store at Perimeter Mall, located off Interstate 285, locally referred to as the Perimeter, at Ashford Dunwoody Road in the northern Atlanta suburb of Dunwoody, Georgia. The three-story, 200,000-plus-square-foot store billed by the company as "The Eighth Wonder of Rich's" contained all the departments offered in Rich's other suburban stores, as well as the restaurant 8th Edition and a separate automotive center in its parking lot.

Within five months of Rich's Perimeter Mall store's opening, management within the company would change for the first time in eleven years. Frank Neely, who had worked at Rich's in various roles over the past forty-eight years and had witnessed Rich's phenomenal growth within the last two decades, officially retired on January 29, 1972, as Rich's honorary chairman of the board. Following his retirement, Dick Rich assumed the role of honorary chairman of Rich's, while Rich's former president Harold Brockey moved into the company's chairman of the board position. Helming the company was Joel Goldberg, who would be the last president of Rich's while it was still family run and who would oversee the firm's transition to that as a division of Federated Department Stores.

Goldberg, a native of Worcester, Massachusetts, and graduate of Dartmouth College, had started his retail career at Filene's before moving to Atlanta and starting at Rich's in the firm as a fashion buyer in 1954. Within seventeen years, he had worked his way up through the ranks of Rich's from buyer to vice-president, then senior vice-president, until becoming the third non-Rich to hold the position of president, a position he would hold for the next six years until Brockey retired and he moved into the role vacated by Brockey, chairman of the board and chief executive officer.

The first large expansion that Goldberg saw as president was the opening of Rich's eighth suburban Atlanta department store in August 1973. This two-story, 200,000-square-foot, Nautilus-themed store opened at Cumberland Mall near the northern suburbs of Vinings and Smyrna, Georgia, and marked the first time that a Rich's opened within a mall that also contained the region's other top three retailers: JCPenney, Davison's and Sears. The store, which contained the Mediterranean fast-food facility Four Corners, a travel bureau, optical department and Photo Reflex portrait studio, had a third level added to it three years after it opened.

Less than a year after the Cumberland store opened, Goldberg saw Rich's create its third nontraditional department store retailing concept, Rich's II.

RICH'S II

After the successes of Rich's Bake Shops and Richway, Rich's tried its hand at yet another retail concept: Rich's II. The boutiques, referred to not only as "Rich's II" but also "II" or "II, a division of Rich's," were small specialty shops specializing in men's and women's sportswear and accessories. The stores were meant to cater to the affluent twenty- to thirty-five-year-old segment of the population and provide a small-shop feeling for those not wanting to shop in traditional department stores or discount department stores. In later years, the stores would expand their merchandise to include non-sportswear clothing, accessories and cosmetics.

The first Rich's II was opened in March 1974 in The Mall at Peachtree Center, a John Portman & Associates–designed shopping center located in

A man peruses items on display inside one of Rich's four Rich's II boutiques, a retailing concept the company introduced in 1974. *Courtesy of Macy's, Inc.*

downtown Atlanta that connected multiple office towers within the greater Peachtree Center complex to one another and was reminiscent of New York City's Rockefeller Center. A second store opened a few months later in the summer of 1974 in Atlanta's mixed-use office-and-hotel Colony Square development. A third store opened in May 1975 at Atlanta's Northlake Mall. The fourth and last Rich's II to open appeared in 1976 at Atlanta's newly opened Omni International Complex (now the CNN Center). This complex was a multiuse office and shopping development that contained the world's first indoor amusement park, The World of Sid and Marty Krofft, and was connected to the Omni Coliseum, an indoor sports and concert arena.[56] The actual store interiors were designed by the Atlanta architectural firm of Stevens & Wilkinson.

While the stores were never that successful, two of them did manage to exist on Atlanta's retail scene for seventeen years. Rich's, owned by Federated since a 1976 merger, was struggling with bankruptcy proceedings and trying to shed debt in 1991 and, therefore, decided to close the stores in March of that year as part of its reorganization efforts. The eleven employees of the Rich's II Peachtree Center and Colony Square boutiques were offered positions at other Rich's locations.

Five months after Rich's had opened its first Rich's II boutique, the company opened its ninth suburban chain department store. This store, however, would not be built in Atlanta but rather in Birmingham, Alabama, marking the first time Rich's left the Atlanta market since the company had moved into Tennessee in 1954 only to pull out in 1961. Opened in August 1974 at Birmingham's Brookwood Village mall, the two-story, 195,000-square-foot store was noted for its slanted glass roof entrance and interior penumbra, a multifaceted canopy of mirrors located between the store's escalators. The store also was noted for its Garden restaurant, which contained eight floral oil paintings Rich's had commissioned from Atlanta artist Comer Jennings.

Less than a year after the Birmingham store opened and in the middle of plans for continued expansion, Rich's lost its iconic leader, Dick Rich. Dick had suffered a stroke in Atlanta and been hospitalized. Eventually, he was transferred to Houston, Texas's Methodist Hospital, where he underwent

Rich's, Inc.—Family Controlled (1929–1976)

Rich's Brookwood Village store opened in 1974 and was the first of three stores to operate within the suburban Birmingham, Alabama area. *Courtesy of Stevens & Wilkinson, Inc.*

a second vascular operation on April 14 at the hands of renowned heart surgeon Dr. Michael DeBakey to help prevent future strokes and to improve his general health. Unfortunately, while recuperating in intensive care after the surgery, Dick died at the age of seventy-three on May 1, 1975, at 4:30 a.m. The death of Atlanta's merchant prince and the grandson of Rich's founder, Morris Rich, came as a shock to the Rich's and Atlanta communities alike; Dick had played a vital role in both for more than fifty years. The day after his death, all Rich's stores, including the bakeries, Richway and Rich's II stores, remained closed in honor of his passing. And while Richites and Atlantans were mourning, Dick's body was brought back to Atlanta and interred at Westview Cemetery next to his wife, Virginia Lazarus of New Orleans, who had died in 1957.

Bookending Dick's death was Rich's second entry into the Birmingham market. In October 1975, the company opened its tenth suburban location, a two-story, sixty-thousand-square-foot store in Century Plaza mall located in the Birmingham suburb of Irondale. This smaller-than-normal Rich's location emphasized ready-to-wear and decorative home furnishings and was run by Marye Bidez, the first female store manager in Rich's history. Despite the store being successful for decades, facing not only competition from tenants within Century Plaza but also from the tenants in Eastwood Mall located across the street, it would close almost thirty years later, making it the fourth Rich's store to close before the company itself ceased to exist.

In the midst of its mid-decade suburban expansions, Rich's also expanded the services it offered at its downtown Atlanta store. In 1975, the company unveiled what would soon be a sizzling hub of activity: Rich's Cooking School.

RICH'S COOKING SCHOOL

By the mid-1970s, Rich's downtown department store, once the epicenter of Atlanta's commerce, was losing customers to its suburban counterparts. The store's corporate food director, Richard Hort, however, thought he had found a way to change that by opening a cooking school and, therefore, hopefully enticing more people to come to the downtown location.

To run the school, Hort had in mind a relatively unknown chef, Nathalie Dupree, whom he had become acquainted with by visiting her restaurant, Mt. Pleasant Village, close to his home, which was located between Covington and Social Circle, Georgia, about a forty-minute drive from Atlanta.[57] Hort also had learned upon his multiple visits to Dupree's restaurant that she had an impressive cooking pedigree, which she used to not only cook and run her restaurant but also to teach cooking classes out of it. Growing up loving to cook but not seriously pursuing her passion until she was an adult, Dupree had enrolled in the renowned Le Cordon Bleu culinary school after she accompanied her first husband to London for a job offer he had received. While at Le Cordon Blue, Dupree met legendary chef Julia Child and asked her what she should do after she obtained her advanced cooking degree. Child, in her warbling, at times falsetto-esque voice, told her to go back to the States, open a cooking school and train people to cook. While the advice was graciously received, it was not acted upon until Dupree had done a stint as a chef in Majorca, Spain, eventually moved back to the States, opened Mt. Pleasant and was approached by Hort to teach at Rich's.

Preparing to embark upon her new career as a full-time cooking instructor, Dupree searched out and then phoned Child, asking her what kind of cooking school she should open at Rich's. Child told her one that was hands-on. Therefore, in September 1975, that is exactly what she did.

Rich's Cooking School was located on the Plaza level of the Store for Homes at Rich's downtown store. There, twenty cooking stations were installed for students to partake in hands-on, full-participation classes. Those classes varied from lunch-and-learns and day courses to a series of courses that lasted a few days, several weeks or several months. Students learned everything from how to make a difficult Bavarian cream or turkey en gelée to something as easy as preparing food for a picnic at an outdoor concert. Occasionally, the school would also hold cooking contests, such as one held in October 1976 using Quaker Oats' new Instant Cheese Grits. The winner of this contest won the "Corny Prize" of a year's supply of grits.

In addition to teaching while at Rich's, Dupree wrote and published her first two cookbooks. Her

Two-time winner of a coveted James Beard Foundation Award, Nathalie Dupree pauses to listen to a student's question while instructing a culinary class at Rich's Cooking School in this 1975 photo. *Courtesy of Macy's, Inc. and Nathalie Dupree.*

first book, *Let's Entertain*, was self-published by Rich's in 1979. Her second book, *Cooking of the South*, was published by chef, author and publisher Irena Chalmers in 1982.

According to Dupree, Rich's Cooking School became "socially centric" over time, with "the center of society coming to it."[58] One could have taken classes with fellow students author Pat Conroy, chef Shirley Corriher or former Atlanta first lady Louise Richardson Allen or been taught by guest chefs Paul Prudhomme, Earl Peyroux or, of course, Julia Child. If none of those individuals happened to be taking the class or teaching it on a given day, one might simply have seen any number of Atlanta's social elite with their sleeves rolled up washing dishes or scrubbing clean a stove top.

Despite the cooking school's social successes and the fact that it had more than ten thousand students over its nearly ten-year run, it was never profitable for Rich's and was closed in late 1984. Dupree's career, however, was not ending but just taking off. She would go on to write her first hardback cookbook, *New Southern Cooking*, as well as ten others; host over three hundred television shows, which have aired on the Food Network, the Learning Channel and PBS; and win two coveted James Beard Foundation Awards.

In addition to adding Rich's Cooking School to the company's downtown Atlanta store, Rich's added a Video Communications Center studio in May 1976. The studio, led by Meg Caruso, would use videotape, new at the time, to record training videos and merchandise presentations, as well as corporate communications. This addition to the downtown store, the store's ever-shrinking space in which to add new facilities, Rich's commitment to maintain a viable presence in downtown Atlanta and the start of construction earlier in the year on Atlanta's rapid-transit hub, MARTA's Five Points Station, across the street from the store prompted company officials to toy with the idea of tearing down the 1924 Store for Fashion and replacing it with a fifty-story office tower. To be built within the next decade, the tower would have a Rich's store in its base and offices on the floors above that. The plan, however, never came to fruition, as Rich's corporate structure would soon change, taking the store in a different direction.

Three months after the Video Communications Center opened, Rich's opened its eleventh suburban store. In August, Rich's two-story, 230,000-square-foot store debuted at Southlake Mall in Morrow, Georgia, a southern suburb of Atlanta located south of the city's airport. Complete with a restaurant and snack bar, the store offered several departments designed in a unique, split-level design.

While the previous six years of the 1970s had been marked with exponential growth for Rich's, the company also was still dedicated to giving back to the patrons who had made it profitable during those and preceding years. In September 1976, Rich's sponsored two events for the delight of its customers in Atlanta: one a charity event and the other an endorsement, and both for sports lovers.

Rich's, Inc.—Family Controlled (1929–1976)

Rich's Porsche 911RS speeds around Road Atlanta's track during its 1976 Camel GT Challenge II five-hundred-kilometer race. *Courtesy of Macy's, Inc.*

From September 13 to 19, Rich's sponsored for the city of Atlanta, as well as tennis lovers from across the country, the United States Tennis Association's (USTA) 1976 Women's Indoor Championships. Held in Atlanta at the Terminus International Tennis Club and the Omni, Chris Evert, Martina Navratilova, Virginia Wade, Evonne Goolagong, Sue Barker, Rosie Casals and others competed for singles and doubles titles. As typical of many of the events Rich's hosted over the years, proceeds raised went to a charity—in this case, the Maureen Connolly Brinker Tennis Foundation of Georgia, Inc., a nonprofit organization that promoted the further development of junior tennis. When the tennis stars were not on the courts, they were visiting Rich's stores, signing autographs, giving demonstrations and mini-matches and hosting tennis clinics.

On the last day of the tennis event, Rich's entered its sponsored Porsche 911RS race car into Road Atlanta's Camel GT Challenge II five-hundred-kilometer race. Rich's car, painted like a tuxedo with "Rich's Tux Shop" on its window and the sides of its hood, "After 6 Formals" on its doors and "Rich's Rents Tuxedos" on its top, was promoting the company's formalities departments. Driven by former Georgia State Wrestling champion Jack Ansley, the car averaged 140 miles per hour and gained two places in the first four laps of the race, but after a hurried pit stop where a faulty transfer coil was discovered, the car flipped over a guard rail in its fifth lap, rolled four times and skidded to a stop. Ansley was unhurt, but the car was demolished. Undeterred by the crash, Rich's sponsored not just another race car three years later but an entire race, Rich's Atlanta Classic, at the Atlanta International Raceway (now Atlanta Motor Speedway), where participating race car drivers included Bobby and Al Unser, Rick Mears and Mike Mosley.

Against these backdrops of tennis and racing, however, was a match of another kind that had recently unfolded and was nearing the finish line—the pairing of Rich's with Federated Department Stores.

Part IV

RICH'S—
FEDERATED OWNED
(1976–2005)

Chapter 11
FEDERATED'S WAY
(1970s)

In July 1976, it was announced to the public that Rich's had agreed to merge with Federated Department Stores, Inc., headquartered in Cincinnati, Ohio, subject to approval by both companies' boards of directors and shareholders. On August 25, the companies' boards of directors approved an Agreement of Merger, whereby shareholders of Rich's would get 0.85 of a share of Federated common stock. On October 25, Rich's stockholders agreed to the merger. The following day, the merger was officially announced to the employees of Rich's, where they were told that Federated had no plans to change Rich's or its policies or to lay off any personnel. Three days later, on October 29, Rich's outstanding shares were converted into 3.5 million shares of Federated common stock, and Rich's ten-thousand-plus employees, twelve department stores, ten Richway stores, three Rich's II boutiques and eleven free-standing bake shops officially became a division of Federated Department Stores.

The merger between Rich's and Federated was a friendly one and deemed as "a pooling of interests."[59] With the merger completed, Rich's, which had been profitable throughout its existence, aligned itself with an industry giant that in time would increase the bank accounts of its stockholders. Federated, on the other hand, capitalized on its previous plans for further expansion and gained entry into the southern United States' retail market. The parent company, formed in 1929 as a federated alliance of department stores, now operated 246 stores in nineteen divisions: Bloomingdale's, Boston Store, Bullock's, Bullock's Northern California, Burdines, Filene's, Foley's, Gold

Circle, Gold Key, Gold Triangle, Goldsmith's, I. Magnin's, Lazarus, Levy's, Ralphs, Rich's, Rike's, Sanger Harris and Shillito's.

While the stockholders of both companies—including the majority of the two company's executive management teams—were happy, not everyone else was pleased with the new corporate structure. Dick Rich's son, Michael P. Rich, who had worked at Rich's since 1962 and at the time of the merger was a vice-president within the organization, objected to the selling off of his family's stores. In fact, he was one of the few who dissented when the board approved the merger in August. Losing the vote to not sell, Michael would eventually leave the company after the merger. Along with Michael, of those not happy with the sale of Rich's were many of its customers, who feared the store would cease to be what it had been under family management.

Change to Rich's as a division of Federated was slow to come at first. But the appointment of Allen I. Questrom to the presidency and Joel Goldberg to the chairman of the board position of Rich's in February 1978, fourteen months after the merger, would be the beginning of numerous personnel changes within the company over the following decades. During Rich's 109 family-controlled years, the store had only six presidents and four chairmen. Under Federated's 29-year control of Rich's, the company would have twelve presidents and ten chairmen. In 1978, however, it was Questrom and Goldberg who led the company into its next stages of growth. By their

Rich's at Columbia Mall opened in 1978 and was the company's first department store in South Carolina. *Courtesy of Stevens & Wilkinson, Inc.*

Opened in 1978, Rich's Augusta Mall location was the chain's thirteenth suburban department store. *Courtesy of Stevens & Wilkinson, Inc.*

side was Harold Brockey, who had retired that February but stayed on for a while, overseeing the continued expansion of Rich's as the chairman of the executive committee.

The first expansion post–Federated and Questrom occurred two months later in April 1978. With the opening of a two-story, 156,000-square-foot store in Columbia Mall in Columbia, South Carolina, Rich's entered into its third retailing market with its twelfth suburban department store. In addition to the store's $46,000 Bosendorfer piano, which customers were invited to play, the store had, within a year of its opening, birds living in the rafters above the Summer Furniture department.

Four months later, Rich's opened its thirteenth suburban department store in its fourth retailing market, Augusta, Georgia. The two-story, 150,000-square-foot store, which only took eleven months to build, opened at the intersection of Bobby Jones Expressway and Wrightsboro Road within Augusta Mall.

Less than a year after the Augusta store opened and ending a decade of massive expansion and corporate acquisition, Rich's former president and chairman of the board, Frank Neely, died at the age of ninety-five on May 24, 1979. Neely was the only executive who saw Rich's progress from Morris Rich's leadership through five presidents, including himself, to become a division of a large retail conglomerate.

Chapter 12

CANADIAN INVASION

(1980s)

Entering into its first new decade no longer under family management but as a division of Federated, Rich's looked forward to increasing its sales and continuing its expansion throughout the region. Rich's was particularly eager to increase sales and foot traffic at its downtown flagship location, which for the last couple of years had seen a decrease in both.

Since 1976, construction on Atlanta's rapid-transit hub, MARTA's Five Points Station, directly across from Rich's downtown store had hampered sales and foot traffic at the location, especially when streets were closed for months at a time for the installation of subway tracks to the new station. Ten days before the start of 1980, however, the station was completed and opened, and it was the hope of Rich's that this would bring people back downtown to shop. Not only could customers now drive to the downtown location with ease as streets were reopened, but they also could ride Atlanta's new subway to the downtown Five Points Station and enter Rich's Store for Fashion via a tunnel connecting the two structures.

With regard to expansion in 1980, Rich's wasted no time in opening new stores. In August of that year, a new Rich's opened in Greenville, South Carolina, and another new Rich's opened in Union City, Georgia, a southern suburb of Atlanta. The Greenville Rich's—at two stories totaling 132,000 square feet—opened at Haywood Mall on Haywood Road near Interstate 385/Golden Strip Freeway and ushered the company into its fourth retail market. The Union City Rich's—at one story totaling 125,000 square feet—opened at Shannon Mall near Jonesboro Road and Interstate 85, south of

Atlanta's airport. This store boasted the distinction of being managed by Rich's first black store manager, Gail Nutt.

By the end of 1980, Rich's had a new president, James "Jim" M. Zimmerman. Zimmerman, who started working at Rich's when he was in college but left the store to work at Foley's and then later worked at Federated's corporate offices and at Sanger-Harris before coming back to Rich's in 1980, was an astute businessman and would eventually leave Rich's to become president and COO of Federated. In addition, however, to possessing savvy business skills that led him up many corporate ladders, Zimmerman strongly believed in giving back to the communities in which he worked. This sense of giving back to the community dovetailed perfectly with Rich's long-standing commitment to do the same, and in 1981, Zimmerman through Rich's helped establish a school for the youth of Atlanta, Rich's Academy.

RICH'S ACADEMY

Exodus, Inc., incorporated in October 1971 and known by many after 1977 as Exodus–Cities In Schools, operated academies in conjunction with Atlanta Public Schools and private organizations throughout the Atlanta area for the purpose of educating high school dropouts and unemployed and troubled youths from ages fourteen to twenty-one. Students at the academies also had access to health services, counseling, legal services, employment assistance, housing assistance and recreational and cultural programs.

As President Ronald Reagan came into office for his first term in 1981, he cut many federally funded programs. He, along with other Republicans, thought many of these federally funded programs were too costly, wasteful and not within the scope of what the government should be involved with. As a result, Exodus, Inc. was left without this much-needed federal funding to run its program.

To rectify this cash shortfall, Exodus's executive director, Neil Shorthouse, also one of its founders, went to Rich's to ask store president Jim Zimmerman for a $25,000 donation. Zimmerman said no to the donation request but said that the downtown Rich's store had lots of available free space that the organization could use and proposed that Exodus house an academy at Rich's. At the suggestion, Shorthouse said on the spot, "Do you mean Rich's Academy?"[60] And thus born at that moment, Rich's Academy joined a roster of several other academies throughout the city—including Academy T, Central Academy, North Avenue Academy, Southside Comprehensive

High School Academy, St. Luke's Academy, Techwood Academy and West End Academy—to teach the city's youth.

Officially opening its doors in 1981 for the 1981–82 school year, the arrangement for Rich's Academy was that Rich's provided space for the school to meet, the Atlanta Public Schools provided the teachers and textbooks for the students and Exodus–Cities In Schools supplied management for the day-to-day operations of the school. Students at the academy, as well as other Exodus academies, were expected to pass a Basic Skills Test, as well as satisfy other requirements established by the Atlanta school board in order to graduate. Successful from the start, Rich's Academy within seven years had 110 students, with a long waiting list for others to get in to the program.

Over time, Rich's would actually not only provide a space for the academy but also would give financial gifts to the school, whether they were from the store's coffers or grants from The Rich Foundation. Additionally, Rich's employees would volunteer at the school in various capacities, while many company executives would serve on Exodus's board and/or volunteer for the organization's annual campaign fund drives. It was also many of these same volunteers who would assist and train students from the academy in jobs they would hold at Rich's, which for many was their first.

Because of the success of the school over the years, Rich's Academy was able to pull in many prominent individuals to speak to its students or visit the school. In April 1985, former First Lady Rosalynn Carter visited the school to observe it in action and talk with its students, encouraging them to finish their education and put in the extra effort it took to be successful in life despite the difficulties they might be facing in their personal lives. A little over a year later, on November 13, 1986, then–Arkansas governor Bill Clinton visited the academy while he was in town for an Education Commission of the States conference, of which he was chairman. Clinton was to tour the school as part of an item agenda for the conference but ended up instead talking to Rich's students for an hour about their lives, which were often fraught with drug abuse, teen pregnancy and unemployment. A few years after Clinton's visit, ABC correspondent Rebecca Chase profiled the academy on an ABC *World News Tonight* show about national dropout prevention programs, and Chrysler chairman Lee Iacocca toured the academy to see if he could use it as a model to set up similar schools across the country through his Iacocca Institute.[61]

Rich's Academy's success also helped it receive many awards over the years, none perhaps as great as the award the school would receive in 1988. On September 29, Rich's chairman and CEO, Roger H. Farah, on behalf of the academy, received the 1988 Presidential Award for Private Sector Initiatives at the White House from the Private Sector Initiative Foundation, which recognized Rich's Academy as one of the thirty best private-sector initiatives in the country. Ironically, the award was presented to Farah by President Ronald Reagan, whose policies seven years earlier had helped create the school.

For nearly ten years, Rich's Academy successfully operated out of Rich's downtown Atlanta store, but in 1991, due to Federated closing the downtown Rich's location in an effort to shed debt and reorganize out of bankruptcy, the academy was moved to the former Bass High School on Euclid Avenue in the Little Five Points area of Atlanta. Once at Bass, Rich's Academy combined with a similar school, Central Academy, already housed at the school and became known as Rich's Central Academy. The following year, Central was shed from the academy's name as the school moved to a building on the George Washington Carver High School campus, where it stayed until the end of the 1993–94 school year. In 1994, the academy moved to spaces within the educational buildings at The Temple, Atlanta's Jewish synagogue on Peachtree Street, where it remained for two school years.

In 1996, the academy was moved yet again by the Atlanta Public School system to Harper-Archer High School in Atlanta, where it was integrated alongside regular public high school classes. This move, however, was not welcomed by all of the participants involved. Exodus–Cities In Schools officials feared that the move to a public high school would threaten the quality of the program, and soon thereafter, their fears were realized when they had difficulty influencing the operation of the program in 1996 as they had in previous years. After the move, Rich's, too, had concerns about the quality and direction the program was headed in and requested that its name be withdrawn from the program's affiliation. Exodus officials, understanding Rich's concerns, had the Atlanta Public School system remove Rich's name from the program, thereby putting an end to the fifteen-year run of Rich's Academy.

Despite pulling its name from the academy in 1996, Rich's continued to provide monetary support to Exodus, which changed its name in 1997 to Communities In Schools to reflect its association with the national organization of the same name. What had been Rich's Academy eventually morphed into the Performance Learning Center and, along with Communities In Schools, became an official part of the school improvement program of the Georgia Department of Education.

Rich's interest in helping the inner-city schoolchildren of Atlanta did not end with the opening of Rich's Academy in 1981. Within a year of its opening, Rich's was involved in Atlanta's Adopt-a-School Program via its affiliation with the Atlanta Partnership of Business & Education, an organization established in 1981 to enhance the quality of education through partnerships between schools, businesses and institutions and an organization that happened to be headed by Rich's president, Jim Zimmerman, in 1982. Through the alliance, Rich's adopted Stanton Elementary School in west Atlanta, where the store and its personnel helped the school upgrade its library and create a school newsletter and assisted in instructional programs, such as student tutoring.

Three years later, Rich's would be involved in a magnet program at Archer High School in Atlanta, where the store initiated the creation of the Archer Center of Retailing. This program, run jointly by Rich's and the Atlanta public school system, prepared students for careers in retailing by giving them hands-on experience. Students took a half day of regular high school classes, followed by a half day of retail-oriented classes, hopefully preparing them for entry-level positions within the retail industry or post-secondary education within a retail field of study.

However, between the opening of Rich's Academy and the opening of the Archer Center of Retailing, Rich's had opened its sixteenth suburban department store at Gwinnett Place mall in Duluth, Georgia, a northern suburb of Atlanta, in February 1984. The two-story, 243,000-square-foot store was unique for Rich's, not because it offered anything the company's other stores did not offer but because it inspired a road name change.

When plans for Gwinnett Place mall were underway and Rich's had committed to build there, Gwinnett County planned on extending Davidson Industrial Way from Beaver Ruin Road north past the new mall. Rich's let the county know that it was not too fond of a road running near its store that sounded similar to its major competitor at the time, Davison's. As a result and to the delight of Rich's executives, the county changed the name of Davidson Industrial Way to Satellite Boulevard in honor and at the suggestion of Collins Radio out of Cedar Rapids, Iowa, which planned to build a plant making rocket components for the U.S. government located off the new road extension. However, before the road extension was completed,

Above: Rich's Gwinnett Place mall store in Duluth, Georgia, opened in 1984 and was the company's sixteenth suburban venue. Its construction sparked the birth of Satellite Boulevard. *Courtesy of Stevens & Wilkinson, Inc.*

Right: Customers shop at Rich's Gwinnett Place jewelry counter in 1984. *Courtesy of Macy's, Inc.*

Collins had become a subsidiary of Rockwell International, which was subsequently purchased by Boeing Integrated Defense Systems years later.[62]

The year following the opening of Rich's Gwinnett Place store, the company embarked on offering many new programs and services to its employees, customers and the general public alike. For Rich's employees, the company launched its Selling Techniques Achieve Results (STAR) program to recognize sales associates who possessed excellent customer service skills. Eventually, the name was changed to Support Techniques Achieve Results (STAR) to incorporate those employees who worked at Rich's but were not in selling positions. For customers in 1985, Rich's installed automated teller machines, known as Richies, on its selling floors and boasted of being the first department store in the country to offer such banking services to its customers. It was, however, the opening of grocery store outlets, a data-processing center and a child-care center that garnered the most attention for Rich's in 1985.

On November 29, 1985, Rich's unveiled its $750,000 investment, J. Bildner & Sons grocery boutique, within its Lenox Square department store location. Over subsequent years, other locations would open in Rich's located in Alabama and Georgia. These grocery stores housed fresh produce, butcher, fish, flower and bakery departments that offered everything from eggs and butter to caviar, pâtés, wild game and other specialty gourmet items. More than ten thousand items stocked the stores' shelves, all marked to be competitive with items at Kroger grocery stores. To purchase the goods, shoppers could use their Rich's credit cards and pay a little extra to have their groceries toted to their car or even delivered to their home. At J. Bildner's fifteen-thousand-square-foot store in Rich's downtown Atlanta location, a customer could also grab a bite to eat within its thirty-two-seat restaurant.

J. Bildner & Sons, a division of Boston-based Windward Management Co., partnered with Rich's in 1985 to not only open grocery boutiques within Rich's department stores but also to manage the company's entire food operations, including multiple snack bars, Magnolia Room restaurants and Rich's catering department and food mail-order operations. However, the partnership was not to last, and within three years, J. Bildner & Sons closed its grocery boutiques and pulled out of Rich's food management, citing operating losses and change-in-business focus as reasons for its sudden departure.

The month after J. Bildner & Sons premiered its grocery store within Rich's Lenox location, Rich's parent company, Federated, created a centralized regional data-processing center in Atlanta to service its Rich's, Burdines and Sanger Harris divisions. This data-processing center, named

SABRE, combined under one roof separate data-processing operations for the three store chains to analyze sales, inventories, credit accounts, personnel information and divisional budgeting. Over time, the center also would use its computers to allocate merchandise within the stores under its support, as well as provide those stores with real-time, online sales and inventory reports and technical support services for in-store registers and computer systems.

SABRE started off with about 120 employees, which quickly swelled to over 800. Nine years after it opened, the data-processing center changed its name to Federated Systems Group (FSG) and was not only processing Federated's department stores data but also competitor Macy's by contract.

While SABRE opened, so, too, did the Downtown Child Development Center, Inc. in Rich's downtown Store for Homes with a soft opening in late 1985 and an official grand opening on February 7, 1986. The center was sponsored by Rich's, Georgia Pacific, the Federal Reserve Bank of Atlanta, First Atlanta Corporation and the *Atlanta Journal-Constitution* and was developed with the assistance of Central Atlanta Progress, a private, nonprofit community development organization that aimed to preserve and strengthen downtown Atlanta. Each of the five companies split the cost to run the facility, with Rich's also donating the 8,700 square feet of space to house it.

Accepting local neighborhood children as well as the children of employees who worked at one of the five sponsoring companies, the center looked after up to 120 children ages twelve weeks to five years between the hours of 7:30 a.m. and 6:30 p.m., Monday through Friday. In addition to nursery facilities, a playground and playrooms, older children were taught counting, fractions, measurements, how to prepare snacks and how to relate to one another within the school facility. Extremely successful from the start, the center soon became a nationwide model for child care. Unfortunately, the center would only remain at Rich's for six and a half years before it was moved to Atlanta's historic Healey Building. Rich's downtown Atlanta complex had been closed, and tenants using space within the vast facility were asked to vacate before construction began on a new federal building on the site.

The month before the Downtown Child Development Center officially opened, Rich's quietly closed its twenty-six-year-old Belvedere store, citing size and configuration limitations as preventing the store from fulfilling its mission as a competitive fashion leader. What also hurt the store were dwindling sales at its registers, as the once middle-class neighborhood surrounding the store had slowly transformed into a less affluent one. The

In 1986, a week after Rich's opened a third store in Birmingham, Alabama, it opened this store at Town Center at Cobb in Kennesaw, Georgia. *Courtesy of Stevens & Wilkinson, Inc.*

store's closure, however, was no setback for Rich's, as a month later, the company opened two new stores within a week of each other.

On February 19, 1986, Rich's opened its third store in the Birmingham, Alabama area. The three-story, 245,000-square-foot store, the largest in the state, opened in Hoover, Alabama, a suburb of Birmingham, just off Interstate 459 in the massive Riverchase Galleria mall, which also contained a fifteen-story hotel and seventeen-story office tower. Seven days later on February 26, Rich's opened a two-story, 235,000-square-foot department store in Town Center at Cobb, a mall sandwiched between Interstates 75 and 575 in the northern Atlanta suburb of Kennesaw, Georgia. These two stores marked the seventeenth and eighteenth suburban department stores, respectively, for the Rich's chain.

Ten months after Rich's opened its two newest department stores, the company ventured into yet another new retailing venture. The company combined its furniture departments from its Lenox Square mall and Perimeter Mall stores and relocated them into a stand-alone building on an outparcel at Perimeter Mall. Opened in December 1986, this new furniture store, dubbed Rich's Furniture Showroom at Perimeter Mall (or Rich's Furniture Showroom), was the first store of its kind to open under the Federated umbrella.

The new ninety-three-thousand-square-foot furniture building contained galleries to showcase Henredon and Connoisseur furniture, as well as other specialty galleries that offered furniture made of leather, wicker and other materials. Also within the store was an interior design studio to assist customers in decorating a home or business, a five-thousand-square-foot furniture clearance center, a credit service department and an auditorium to be rented for special events or community meetings by local organizations.

When the store opened, it was done so by Rich's and Federated as an experiment to see if the company could increase its furniture sales. The experiment paid off, and within six months of opening, the store had increased sales by 69 percent over the formerly two separate furniture locations that were housed within the Lenox and Perimeter Rich's stores.

Just a little over a year after Rich's Furniture Showroom opened, an unexpected suitor would make a bid for Federated, which would throw both Rich's and its corporate parent into turmoil. Little did either of them know that the machinations behind the unexpected bid had started the same year that the two were celebrating their new furniture venture.

On October 31, 1986, French Canadian real estate mogul Robert Campeau signed an agreement to merge his company, Campeau Corporation, with that of Allied Store Corporation, the parent company of Brooks Brothers, Jordan Marsh and others. This agreement to merge came only after a hostile leveraged buyout from Campeau of Allied, which he wanted in order to provide anchor stores for retailing establishments he intended to build in the United States.

After obtaining Allied, Campeau turned his sights on Federated, a much larger "prize" than Allied. Prompting Campeau to move quickly on obtaining Federated were reports that Donald Trump intended to purchase fifteen million of the company's shares and that an anti-takeover statute was on the verge of passing in Delaware, where most American companies incorporated. Therefore, in the summer and fall of 1987, Campeau started buying large blocks of Federated stock through a dummy corporation that he had set up in a movement his camp dubbed "Project Rose," named so after Cincinnati's famous baseball player Pete Rose.

By January 1988, Campeau had purchased approximately 400,200 shares of Federated stock and decided to offer Federated on January 25 $4.2 billion, or $47 a share in cash, for 90 million shares of Federated stock, despite the fact that he had no funding to do so. On February 4, Federated's board of directors rejected Campeau's bid. After being rebuffed by Federated, Campeau arranged financing for the takeover with loans from the Edward J. DeBartolo Corp. of

Ohio and the wealthy Canadian Reichmann family, as well as the selling off of Allied's Brooks Brothers department store for a huge profit. As a result, he again approached Federated's board twice in February with increased bid amounts in the hopes of taking over the company but was turned down each time. Finally, Federated agreed at the end of the month to meet with Campeau to discuss a possible merger once his bid hit $6.1 billion, or $68 a share in cash. A few days later, however, on March 2, Federated agreed to be acquired instead by R.H. Macy & Co., acting as a white knight, for $74.50 a share.

While Campeau, Macy's and Federated argued in court over competing offers and "poison pill" defenses during the month of March, Rich's management in Atlanta was exploring the possibility of buying Rich's from Macy's or Campeau if either of them succeeded in acquiring Federated; this plan, however, was never executed. By March 29, Federated had asked Macy's and Campeau to put their final offers on the table in an effort to end the bidding battle, which had been deemed too distracting for the company's employees. Over the next two days, Campeau and Macy's attempted to win over Federated with sweetened deals, to no avail.

On March 31, Campeau met with Macy's president, Edward S. Finkelstein, at 7:00 p.m. in his Manhattan town house on 77th Street to discuss each other's acquisition attempts and to hopefully iron out a deal between the two. After a three-hour meeting, the two reached an agreement, and the two-month fight for Federated was over. Macy's agreed to drop out of the bidding in exchange for the opportunity to buy Federated's I. Magnin, Bullocks and Bullock's Wilshire chains, which would allow Macy's entry into the West Coast. The company would also be paid $60 million for legal and investment banking fees it incurred in its takeover attempts. Campeau, on the other hand, emerged from the meeting victorious, offering to pay $73.50 a share, or $6.6 billion, to acquire Federated. The following day, April Fool's Day, Federated agreed to Campeau's offer, making the merger at that time the largest in U.S. retail history.

While the finalities of the buyout were being worked out, Campeau made trips to several of his newly acquired department stores throughout the country during the month of April. One of those trips brought him to Rich's downtown Atlanta store, where from the Magnolia Room, he told gathered employees that they should not be concerned about losing their jobs or fear store closings; he actually had plans to expand the chain. Unfortunately, this was not to hold true for many of Federated's divisions, including Rich's.

In May, when Campeau formally took control of his newly acquired company, he immediately started to dismantle and rearrange it. As promised, he sold Bullock's, Bullock's Wilshire and I. Magnin to Macy's, followed by the sale of Foley's and Filene's to May Department Stores, the parent company of the Hecht Company, Lord & Taylor and other stores. Later, Federated's Richway stores, not a part of Rich's for eight years, and Gold Circle stores were sold to Dayton Hudson Corp.'s Target Stores.

Cuts at Rich's starting in May and June included employee layoffs, which affected 250 people in positions ranging from corporate jobs to clerical and sales jobs. Additionally, Campeau closed the budget departments at four stores, cut back operating hours at some locations, reduced management travel and trimmed advertising budgets. The biggest change Rich's would notice, however, was the folding of Federated's Memphis-based Goldsmith's division into its own in the fall of 1988. The new division—Rich's/Goldsmith's—would be operated from Atlanta and would consist of all of Rich's stores in Alabama, Georgia and South Carolina, as well as six Goldsmith's department stores located in Tennessee.

While Rich's and its corporate parent, Federated, were making headlines across the country in newspapers about their recent acquisition and subsequent events, Rich's was also making an appearance on national television. On June 26, 1988, the story of the murder of Rich's security guard London "Bruno" Johnson aired to an estimated fifteen million viewers on *America's Most Wanted*. Johnson had been fatally stabbed at Rich's downtown Atlanta store five months earlier when he tried to apprehend a man and woman suspected of shoplifting. In an effort to capture the two individuals still on the run, show producers came to Atlanta early in June and spent two days filming at Rich's downtown store to re-create the events surrounding the murder. It was the hopes of the producers, Rich's executives and Atlanta police that when the show aired, someone watching it would recognize the two suspects and phone in tips to the producers of their whereabouts. Five days later, that is exactly what happened when two phone calls led police in St. Louis, Missouri, to the individuals on the run; both suspects were quickly arrested and brought to justice.

The camera crews that June were not the first time cameras had rolled at Rich's during the decade. A year earlier, actress Candice Bergen had been filmed in the store portraying Sydney Biddle Barrows, a real-life madam and descendant of the *Mayflower* settlers, for the CBS made-for-television movie *Mayflower Madam*. Sadly, too, London Johnson was not the only person murdered at Rich's in the 1980s. Three years earlier, off-duty Atlanta police officer and part-time Rich's security guard Philip Bruce Mathis was shot and killed when he surprised a burglar in a storeroom at Rich's Lenox Square store. Five years before his murder, Fay Garrison, a part-time employee at the post office located within Rich's downtown Atlanta store, was shot and killed during a cash-drawer robbery.

In direct contrast to Rich's employees being victims of crimes, Rich's initiated a program to help combat crime. In September 1988, Wilton Gore, a security and credit manager at Rich's Town Center at Cobb store, helped Rich's, along with Cobb County, Georgia officials, establish the Cobb County Teen Court. The court, a community-based alternative to the formal court process for alleged youthful offenders, consisted of an all-teen jury that handed out punishment to first-time offenders ages thirteen to seventeen convicted of crimes ranging from shoplifting and vandalism to disorderly conduct and underage alcohol possession. The teens involved in the organization also acted as prosecutors, defense attorneys, bailiffs and clerks. An official Cobb County judge oversaw the sentences handed down by the teen jury. A success within its first year, the court won a 1989 Achievement Award from the National Association of Counties, while Gore won a national community action award from Federated/Allied for his efforts.

Seven months after Rich's helped establish the Cobb County Teen Court, the company would start another volunteer entity, Partners in Time. This program would quickly go on to garner more press for its good deeds than almost any other program created by Rich's or Federated combined.

PARTNERS IN TIME

Rich's always had a long history of supporting charitable causes and donating money from either its store coffers or from its charitable organization, The Rich Foundation. By 1989, however, things had changed. As a result of the hostile takeover of Rich's parent company, Federated Department Stores, a year earlier and the subsequent debt acquired and bad business decisions made thereafter, money was tight. Federated was headed for bankruptcy, and the large amount of money once given to support various charitable causes or groups was being reduced or stopped altogether. As a result, Rich's divisional vice-president of community affairs, Carol Dunlap Reiser, came up with the idea of creating a volunteer program, Partners in Time, where the store's employees would donate free labor to make up for the loss in actual dollars normally given out by the store to various groups.[63]

Reiser, who was born in New York, lived in numerous places throughout her life and graduated from the University of Colorado, moved to Atlanta

Started in 1989 by Carol Dunlap Reiser, Rich's Partners in Time employee volunteer program quickly spread throughout all of Federated Departments Stores' divisions and continues to operate through Macy's. *Courtesy of Macy's, Inc.*

in 1975 and started working at Rich's in 1979. She was no stranger to volunteer work and seemed to have a passion for it, having helped establish the Corporate Volunteerism Council of Atlanta and serving on the boards of Families First, the YWCA of Greater Atlanta, the Foundation for Hospital Art, the Wellness Community, Young Audiences, the Points of Light Foundation's Council for Workplace Volunteerism and the Penn Center, a South Carolina school for African Americans created in 1862 by abolitionists. It was only natural that she would marry her passion with her job at Rich's.

Reiser's creation, Partners in Time, debuted on Saturday, April 22, 1989, in conjunction with suburban Atlanta's Gwinnett County Walk-a-Thon titled "Walk Like a Gwinnettian," a play on the 1986 number-one hit song "Walk Like an Egyptian" by the Bangles. The group of twenty Partners in Time volunteers from Rich's Gwinnett Place mall store and Rich's Service Center handed out sodas and hot dogs to over ten thousand walkers from a stand set up at a local school near the eight-mile mark along the twelve-mile course. Sponsored by the Gwinnett County Board of Education, the walk-a-thon raised over $350,000 to establish a trust fund to help defray the future operating costs of Gwinnett County's twelve-bed children's shelter, which had opened the previous year.

After the Gwinnett County Walk-a-Thon, Rich's Partners in Time volunteers quickly lent their time to other projects in Atlanta, such as planting more than three thousand bulbs in Zoo Atlanta's flower beds; visiting children at local hospitals; working with Kroger groceries, WAGA-TV and Federal

Express in Project Overcoat, a program that provided warm clothing for the homeless; or working along with the Foundation for Hospital Art to create murals for local hospitals. With the program's success in Atlanta, which created quite a buzz in the press for Rich's, it quickly spread to Goldsmith's in Tennessee, Rich's new divisional partner under Federated. By the fall of 1989, Goldsmith's Partners in Time program was organized and out doing good within the Memphis area. Soon thereafter, the program spread to all Rich's/Goldsmith's stores located within Alabama, Georgia, South Carolina and Tennessee, and by the end of its first year, Partners in Time had racked up more than 4,500 volunteer hours.

Additional projects that Partners in Time volunteers gave their time to over subsequent years were volunteering for Special Olympics events; collecting donations for AIDS walks; creating valentines for seniors in care facilities and children in hospitals; and renovating homes, schools and homeless shelters. Other projects included delivering and decorating Christmas trees for community organizations, installing playground equipment, assisting with food drives, helping local Shriner's hospitals with various activities at Christmas, helping school systems with their Adopt-a-School programs, hosting fashion shows for the elderly at nursing homes or volunteering at Festival of Trees events that benefited local hospitals.

Some of these endeavors drew huge numbers. In 1990, approximately four hundred Rich's employees converged at the Chattahoochee River National Recreation Area north of Atlanta to help shore up and stabilize the river's banks. Three years later, one hundred Rich's Partners in Time volunteers would help rebuild and raise a 450-foot section of a boardwalk, renovate a classroom and help clean up wetland and woodland trails at the Chattahoochee Nature Center in Roswell, Georgia, a facility visited by over sixty thousand school kids each year.

By 1997, Federated had taken notice of Rich's/Goldsmith's Partners in Time programs and the impact they were making on the communities they served. Through Reiser, Federated implemented the program throughout all its divisions across the country and watched the program prosper, doing good not only in Atlanta but also in the neighborhoods of New York City, Cincinnati, San Francisco and elsewhere. Unfortunately, five years after Reiser helped Federated expand the program and just eight days after she retired from Rich's to devote time to writing children's books, she died unexpectedly of complications from pneumonia at the age of fifty-one.

Fortunately for countless charity organizations across the country, Reiser's legacy of volunteerism lives on in the program she created. In 2007,

Federated changed its name to Macy's, Inc., and to this day Partners in Time continues as its nationwide employee volunteerism program and is recognized as among the best in corporate America. In 2005, the program received for its efforts the Points of Light/Hands On Network Award for Excellence in Workplace Volunteerism. Since its inception, more than 1.9 million hours of community service, valued as a $32 million contribution to those served, have been logged.[64]

Unfortunately, just as Partners in Time was spreading throughout Campeau's newly created division of Rich's/Goldsmith's, he was losing control of his retail empire consisting of Federated and Allied. By 1989, Federated and Allied were operating at a loss. The companies had too many outstanding debts, upward of $7.9 billion, and suppliers, who were afraid of not getting paid, stopped supplying goods to their stores, including Rich's. By September 1989, Campeau was forced to turn over control of Federated and Allied to a committee on the Campeau Corporation Board of Directors. Two months later, Campeau's creditors were seeking to restructure Federated and Allied outside of court, but by mid-month, Federated and Allied had announced that they had a severe cash crunch problem and that they might soon have to seek bankruptcy protection.

Fortunately for Rich's, an event held in December of that year deflected some of the negative press and possible bankruptcy plans of its parent corporation—*Gone with the Wind*'s fiftieth film anniversary. The weeklong event held December 10–15 was organized by Turner Home Entertainment, a division of Turner Broadcasting System, and included several events throughout Atlanta and neighboring cities, including memorabilia exhibits, tours, lectures, a look-a-like contest, balls and *Gone with the Wind* film screenings twice a day at CNN Cinemas 6 at the CNN Center in downtown Atlanta. The Atlanta Historical Society premiered the *"Gone with the Wind*: The Facts About the Fiction" exhibit, which hosted many artifacts about the making of the movie, its premiere and movie memorabilia, including the white coat Margaret Mitchell purchased at Rich's for the December 15, 1939 film premiere at Loew's Grand in downtown Atlanta. The entire weeklong celebration ended with a re-premiere of the movie held at Atlanta's Fox

Theatre, which was hosted by Larry King and included the appearance of some of the original cast members from the movie.

For Rich's, however, the pièce de résistance was its hosting of the official *Gone with the Wind* cast reunion party on December 13 at 8:00 p.m. in its downtown Atlanta store. The event was for invited guests only and held at the store's Polo department and fine fragrance area. Cast members Ann Rutherford (Carreen O'Hara), Butterfly McQueen (Prissy), Atlanta-born Evelyn Keyes (Suellen O'Hara), Patrick Curtis (infant Beau Wilkes), Greg Geiss (baby Bonnie Blue Butler), Cammie King Conlon (older Bonnie Blue Butler), Mickey Huhn (Beau Wilkes) and Rand Brooks (Charles Hamilton) talked to those gathered about the movie, its impact on their lives and how quickly it seemed the last fifty years had gone by. The following day, the cast members reappeared at the store for an hour to meet the general public in the Store for Fashion's cosmetics area.

Chapter 13

BACK FROM THE BRINK

(1990s)

Fifteen days into the new decade, Rich's parent company, Federated Department Stores, Inc., along with Allied Store Corporation (known together as Campeau Corp. U.S.), filed for federal bankruptcy protection in Cincinnati, Ohio, Federated's headquarters. In doing so, the two brought about the largest bankruptcy filing in American retail history up until that time. The ill-fated, over-leveraged venture of Robert Campeau into the U.S. retailing market eighteen months earlier was to blame. Federated and Allied were choking on more than $7 billion in debt, and it was the hope that bankruptcy protection would set the stage for an overhaul of Campeau's department store chains.

The day after Federated filed bankruptcy, January 16, 1990, Rich's placed a full-page letter in the *Atlanta Journal-Constitution* telling its customers that the store was operating as usual; however, on the minds of not just Rich's executives but also the company's staff that day and for months later was what the future held for the store. Some thought that the restructuring of Federated and Allied under bankruptcy protection might mean that Rich's would be put on the selling block. If so, it was made known that May Department Stores, the parent of Loehmann's and Lord & Taylor's, as well as an Atlanta private investor group led by The Robinson-Humphrey Company, Inc., might be interested in buying the chain. The placement of Rich's for sale, however, never materialized.

What did happen at Rich's after the bankruptcy filing was the elimination of 156 jobs in its credit division, which was relocated to a regional center near Cincinnati. These layoffs marked the second-largest cutback by Rich's in its history, both of which occurred as a result of Campeau. A few months later, 56 jobs were eliminated at Rich's Stone Mountain Service Center when its drapery workroom was closed. Officially, Rich's executives stated the layoffs had nothing to do with its parent company's bankruptcy issues. Also nixed at Rich's as a result of Federated's bankruptcy was its plans to open stores in Asheville and Charlotte, North Carolina.

Despite being constrained by a shortage of cash as a result of bankruptcy, Rich's managed to donate money, along with Coca-Cola Enterprises, Cox Enterprises, Delta Air Lines, Georgia Power Co. and others, toward the construction of a $2.7 million museum at Underground Atlanta, an entertainment complex opened a year earlier in the underground spaces created by the construction of street viaducts in downtown Atlanta in the 1920s. The museum, Atlanta Heritage Row, opened on September 15, 1990, and told the history of Atlanta.

Perhaps what allowed Rich's a little extra money to donate to the museum was the money it was earning by leasing spaces in its downtown Atlanta's Store for Homes to Fulton County as a place for temporary courtrooms. Four months earlier, in May, Fulton County judges started to dispense justice from two temporary courtrooms set up in the Store for Homes to ease overcrowding at Atlanta's nearby Superior Court building. One of the courtrooms was used for domestic relations cases, while the other was used for longer-running civil trials. Both, which had cost $100,000 to build, were experimental in design and allowed judges to give feedback on the way they wanted their new courtrooms to be designed in the city's soon-to-be-built justice center.

In spite of the good Rich's had done in the second half of 1990, it would all be overshadowed by the news on April 18, 1991, that the company's 1924 flagship store and surrounding buildings had been put up for sale. For $12 million, someone could buy the 5.15-acre, two-city-block site that contained 1.2 million square feet of space, equivalent to the space within Atlanta's fifty-five-story Bank of America Plaza building at North Avenue and Peachtree Street. Officially, company management attributed the closure of the store to Rich's parent company's ongoing bankruptcy problems and to the fact that the store had been losing money for the past five years. Unofficially, the store had become a victim of competition, corporate restructuring and white flight. The downtown Rich's actually stayed open much longer than similar stores from other chains. Hudson's closed its flagship store in Detroit in 1982, as Elder-Beerman and Ayres did in Cincinnati in 1985 and 1988, respectively, and Gimbels did in New York City in 1986.

Rich's—Federated Owned (1976–2005)

The announcement that Rich's would be closing its venerable downtown store prompted the *Atlanta Journal-Constitution* to set up a special hotline for people to call in and record their memories of the store. More than two hundred people did just that, although not everyone in Atlanta felt the same about the store or its past. White customers reminisced about the good times they had at the store riding the Pink Pigs and eating in the Magnolia Room, while black customers remembered the store for its segregation policies. Besides the memories, people also commented on what the abandoned store might be used for—dorms for students attending Georgia State University, a multimodal train station, a discount center or an art school. On April 21, *Atlanta Journal-Constitution* columnist and humorist Lewis Grizzard even wrote a column about the store's closure, how his father had sold shirts there and that his first-ever autograph session was within its walls.

Not three months after it was announced that the store was closing, its doors were locked to the public at 6:00 p.m. on July 13. The 242 store employees who had worked at that store were offered jobs at other Rich's. Over 700 Rich's/Goldsmith's office personnel housed within the store complex remained on site until they were moved into two new office buildings near Perimeter Mall north of downtown Atlanta six months later. The store's Finale clearance center was moved to Rich's Greenbriar Mall store, while its photo studio and other departments were relocated from downtown to Rich's Service Center in Stone Mountain. The store's sixty-seven years as the retail heart of Atlanta were over.

Ironically, eleven days after Rich's had announced to the Atlanta public that it was closing its downtown store, Federated and Allied filed a plan of reorganization with the U.S. Bankruptcy Court in Cincinnati to hopefully resurrect the company. Within the reorganization, Federated and Allied would cut all ties to Campeau and his corporation and merge into one publicly traded company, Federated Department Stores, Inc. The new company would issue shares, along with cash and other debt instruments, to fulfill obligations to its creditors. Eight months later in December, Federated and Allied's creditors approved the plan, and a month after that, it went before U.S. Bankruptcy judge J. Vincent Aug Jr. for confirmation and approval. On January 10, he agreed to Federated and Allied's plan and signaled that they could exit bankruptcy in early February.

On February 5, 1992, when Federated Department Stores, Inc. officially exited bankruptcy protection, stocks on Wall Street soared. For Rich's approximately eight thousand employees, Federated's exit meant job security, when months earlier the closure of Rich's downtown Atlanta store might

Rich's Oglethorpe Mall store opened in Savannah, Georgia, in 1992, ending the decades-long practice of many Savannahians driving to shop at the company's Atlanta store. *Courtesy of Stevens & Wilkinson, Inc.*

have signaled otherwise. Despite the new company being slimmer than it had been when Campeau took over its reins, it was on the rebound and would quickly prosper. Even while in bankruptcy protection, both Rich's and other Federated divisions had shown ever-increasing profits from sales.

Proof of Rich's financial health after Federated exited bankruptcy manifested itself less than a year later when Rich's opened its nineteenth suburban department store in Savannah, Georgia, at Oglethorpe Mall in September 1992. For more than one hundred years, Savannahians had trekked the approximately 250 miles from Savannah to Atlanta either by rail (for twenty-two of those years by way of the Nancy Hanks train) or by car to shop at Rich's. Now, they had their own two-story, 135,000-square-foot store to patronize. Within the first four days of the store's opening, registers had tallied $944,000 in sales. By the end of the store's first week in business, one thousand credit accounts had been opened, joining the twenty-five thousand Rich's credit card holders already living in Savannah.

Exactly a year after Rich's opened its Savannah store, the company opened another store at North Point Mall in Alpharetta, Georgia, a northern suburb of

Rich's—Federated Owned (1976–2005)

The North Point Mall Rich's opened in 1993. It was designed with replicas of Rich's famous clock found at its 1924 Atlanta flagship store and bas-relief sculptures portraying different periods in the company's history. *Courtesy of Macy's, Inc.*

Atlanta, in September 1993, a month before the mall officially opened. This two-story, 240,000-square-foot store, Rich's twentieth suburban department store, was architecturally different than most of the other stores Rich's had opened over the past thirty-plus years. Typically speaking, Rich's had opened modern, utilitarian stores devoid of much architectural detailing on their façades. The North Point Mall store, however, was designed to harken back to the more ornate style of downtown department store locations found throughout the country. On the exterior of this store at each of its three outside entrances were replicas of Rich's famous clock that adorned the corner of the former 1924 flagship store. Also, the store had eight niches along its sides, where traditional show windows would have existed, that contained bas-relief sculptures portraying different periods in the then 126-year history of Rich's.

Nine months after the North Point Mall Rich's opened, an eleven-year-old asthma patient from Hughes Spalding Children's Hospital at Grady pushed a button at 7:30 a.m. on June 5, 1994, that imploded the Store for Homes at Rich's old downtown Atlanta site. The demolition, insured by Lloyds of London for $10 million, was the start of construction on the former Rich's site that would eventually house the Sam Nunn Atlanta Federal Center, which, when completed four years later, would have over 1.5 million square feet of office space in it to house over five thousand federal workers. To the delight of preservationists throughout the city of Atlanta, part of the complex would contain Rich's 1924 building restored back to its original grandeur; it had escaped the wrecking ball. To the dismay of civil rights participants and historians, the Crystal Bridge spanning Forsyth Street between the Store for Homes and Store for Fashion was not spared destruction.

A view of Rich's 1924 flagship store as part of the Sam Nunn Atlanta Federal Center. The store, the office tower behind it and other surrounding buildings house office spaces for federal workers. *Courtesy of Stevens & Wilkinson, Inc.*

As part of construction requirements on any site where federal money is involved, Congress required that studies be done and archaeological digs be conducted to find and preserve as many artifacts as possible. Two years before the demolition of the Store for Homes had occurred, archaeologists were hired to study the history of the old Rich's site. After the rubble was cleared from the demolition, an actual archaeological dig was conducted there. Both yielded tantalizing histories and artifacts.

The two-year study on the Rich's site revealed that the Store for Homes had been built on top of part of the National Pencil Co. factory, which played host to one of the most notorious murders in Atlanta's history. It was at the factory in 1913 that thirteen-year-old factory worker Mary Phagan was murdered, with the blame placed on the factory's Jewish superintendent, Leo Frank. Phagan's death and Frank's subsequent lynching spawned the Knights of Mary Phagan and the birth of the Anti-Defamation League of B'nai B'rith. It was also discovered that the site at one point in time contained the original Atlanta Fire Station No. 1, as well as old "Negro tenements," middle-class businesses, livery stables, bars, poolrooms, a brewery, boardinghouses and a red-light district.

The archaeological dig at the site, which was conducted by R.S. Webb & Associates and lasted about a month, unearthed—literally—more than seven thousand artifacts, of which many had been found in an old well long covered over and forgotten. While many of the artifacts—old knives, forks, a Blue Jasperware teapot, chamber pots, toys, bottles, porcelain doll remnants, marbles, doorknobs, inkwells and tobacco pipes—were fascinating and offered a glimpse into old Atlanta, one was downright dangerous: a live, undetonated Hotchkiss Yankee (Union Hotchkiss) artillery shell from the American Civil War. The shell, which weighed twelve pounds and contained fifteen lead balls designed to inflict severe bodily harm, was quickly detonated by Atlanta Police SWAT.

Just a little over six months after Rich's Store for Homes was imploded, Federated acquired Macy's on December 19, 1994, for approximately $3.8 billion. With the acquisition of Macy's, Federated now had more than 450 stores, including Rich's, in thirty-five states with more than 110,000 sales associates. Ironically, the acquisition of Macy's marked a reversal in fortune for the company. In 1988, it was Macy's that had tried to take over Federated from Robert Campeau. However, the deal Macy's made with Campeau to buy Bullock's, Bullock's Wilshire and I. Magnin, coupled with the debt Macy's had incurred two years prior to that with a senior-management buyout, actually led to the retailer's downfall.

Overladen with billions of dollars in debt, Macy's entered into bankruptcy protection nine days before Federated emerged from it in 1992. Two years later, Federated acquired $449.3 million for half of Macy's secured debt, which had been owned by Prudential Insurance Company of America. The acquisition of this debt was not viewed by Federated as a hostile attempt to take over Macy's but an attempt to combine the chains to compete against the ever-growing rise of discount retailers, wholesale clubs and catalogue retailers. Initially, Macy's had been resistant to the acquisition attempts of Federated, but in July 1994, the retailer finally relented and agreed to the merger, which when completed in December of that year pulled it out of bankruptcy and made it a division of Federated.

The effects of Federated's acquisition of Macy's were twofold on Rich's. First, Rich's had competed against Macy's in Atlanta since 1925, when the company had bought Davison's, which it renamed Macy's in 1985. Now, the two rival stores were owned by the same parent company and were located together in several malls throughout the South. Second, Federated in early 1995 started to realign store divisions operating under its control and in March began consolidating Cincinnati-based Lazarus department stores into Rich's/Goldsmith's division. Lazarus had been established in Cincinnati in 1851 and by the time of the Macy's acquisition operated fifty stores throughout the Midwest.

By June, Rich's/Goldsmith's had become Rich's/Lazarus/Goldsmith's. To create this division, Federated closed Lazarus's Cincinnati central offices and moved them to Atlanta. The new division operated seventy-five stores under three different nameplates in nine states, all of which were managed from Atlanta via an executive management team. In addition to the combining of Lazarus into Rich's/Goldsmith's at this time, Federated had combined its Abraham & Strauss/Jordan Marsh division into Macy's East, converting nine Abraham & Strauss stores to the Macy's nameplate, signaling a trend the company would follow over the next decade at all of its stores.

A year later, Federated, in owning both Rich's and Macy's, cornered the Atlanta retailing market in exposing millions of visitors to its wares when the city hosted the 1996 Centennial Olympic Summer Games from July 19 to August 4. While Rich's downtown store had closed five years earlier, Macy's downtown Atlanta store was still operating in the heart of the city on Peachtree Street. There, foreign visitors were greeted by foreign-exchange students employed from area universities to act as interpreters and sales associates. Additionally, the Macy's store offered extended shopping hours; an in-store convention and visitors' bureau; foreign currency exchange; and special shipping and delivery services to visitors' home countries. Rich's, however, was not left out of the Olympic fever simply because its downtown store was gone. It, as did Macy's, offered visitors to its suburban Atlanta stores "Olympic" shops from which to buy officially licensed Olympic merchandise, as well as multilingual currency and apparel size-conversion signs for the ease of buying goods throughout its stores.

Even before foreign visitors came to Atlanta that summer, Rich's had been involved in special Olympic events in anticipation of the games, such as the February 23, 1996 presentation of the "Olympic Dream Tour." Held in Rich's Lenox Square store parking lot, this tour, sponsored by Chevrolet, involved the display of $3 million worth of Olympic memorabilia, including medals, torches and uniforms from the first modern Olympics held in 1896 up until the 1992 games held in Barcelona, Spain. The event also included a movie—*The Olympic Dream*, shown in a tent outside the store and presented by the U.S. Olympic Committee—and a forty-foot backlit photography wall with memorable moments from past games on display. A little over a month later, on March 28, Rich's Lenox Square store hosted five gold-medal Olympic athletes—swimmer Mark Spitz, speed skater Dan Jansen and track and field competitors Edwin Moses, Daley Thompson and Bob Beamon—in its store to promote the launch of Swatch Watch's Olympic Legends collection.

Ironically, Rich's received more press in regards to the Olympics not because of its voluntary involvement but because of thefts that occurred at its Lenox Square store by two Armenian Olympic wrestlers. The two athletes, Araik Bagdadian and Armen Simonian, were arrested for shoplifting $136 worth of clothing from the store in August 1995 while they were in Atlanta for pre-Olympic competition. They were released on their own recognizance after their arrests when officials from the Atlanta Committee for the Olympic Games intervened on their behalf. However, instead of appearing at a local court hearing the day after their release, the two absconded back to Armenia. They were reportedly told they could send a representative to court to pay fines, which was not the case. Back in Armenia, the law caught up with them, and the duo spent two weeks in an Armenian jail. They were then removed from Armenia's Olympic team, lost their living stipends and were publicly chastised. Five months before the Olympics kicked off in Atlanta, an Armenian representative paid the fines incurred by the two in a Fulton County court.

A year after the Olympics, Federated debuted its national gift registry in 1997. The computerized system, developed at Federated Systems Group (FSG) in Norcross, Georgia, allowed bridal couples or anyone else to use handheld scanners to scan merchandise barcodes throughout Rich's or other selected Federated stores throughout the country to compile a gift registry list. This list was then available at any store throughout the country, allowing friends or relatives to buy gifts in another city or state for the person who compiled the list. Additionally, on October 6 of that year, Rich's opened a Piedmont Hospital Mammography Center on the third floor of its Rich's Perimeter Mall store. This center, the first one in a department store in Georgia, allowed female customers to have a mammogram done, which, if they wanted, could be charged to their Rich's credit cards.

In January 1998, over a decade after Rich's opened its then-new retailing concept, Rich's Furniture Showroom at Perimeter Mall, the company opened its second furniture showroom at Gwinnett Place mall. This fifty-thousand-square-foot store, like its predecessor, was in a separate building apart from Rich's department store at the mall and would cater exclusively to special lines of furniture. The Gwinnett Place mall department store also went through a significant change at this time when its individual registers were done away with and replaced with large checkout centers (or stations) installed at various junctures of departments within the store. A few years later, this concept, albeit in a slightly different form, would be tried out at other Rich's department stores.

Rounding out the 1990s, a decade of vast extremes—from bankruptcy to acquirer—Federated rebranded two Macy's stores, converting them into Rich's and giving the chain its twenty-first and twenty-second department stores. On June 27, 1998, the Macy's store at Macon Mall in Macon, Georgia, and the Macy's store at Georgia Square Mall in Athens, Georgia, closed. The following day, the two stores reopened as Rich's in cities that had long wanted them and in cities that Rich's had long eyed to enter.

Chapter 14

WITHOUT FANFARE

(2000s)

The fear that Y2K, or the Millennium Bug, would wreak havoc on computer systems worldwide on January 1, 2000, and cause the possible collapse of businesses across the globe was largely unfounded. Rich's/Lazarus/Goldmsith's, as well as Federated Department Stores, entered the new millennium unscathed from the much-hyped event with its computer systems intact, strong sales—approximately $2 billion and $17 billion, respectively—and an eye toward capitalizing on the ever-growing use of the Internet. Federated, via Macy's, had a limited online presence since 1996 but launched a full-fledged Internet site for Macy's, Macy's.com, in 1998. This site offered a limited selection of cosmetics, accessories and high-priced clothing. A site like this for Rich's, however, had eluded the company until after Y2K.

On January 26, 2000, Rich's debuted Richsonline.com. The site, developed in conjunction with Cox Interactive Media, a unit of Cox Enterprises, offered limited selections of merchandise and downloadable coupons for select items but was never really a full-fledged Internet buying site like Macy's.com. Instead, Rich's website was primarily used as a vehicle from which to market to Rich's customers, providing them incentives to visit their local Rich's department stores in person.

After debuting Richsonline.com, the company turned back to its tried-and-true retail ventures with the opening of its third furniture showroom. Rich's North Point Furniture Showroom opened in July 2000 at Mansell Crossing shopping center adjacent to North Point Mall in the affluent

Above: Rich's "time after time" logo in the early 2000s as it appeared on a shirt box top. *Courtesy of Macy's, Inc.*

Left: Rich's twenty-third suburban department store at the Mall of Georgia opened in 2000. The company had not planned to build at the mall until it discovered Nordstrom was erecting a store there. *Courtesy of Stevens & Wilkinson, Inc.*

northern Atlanta suburb of Alpharetta, Georgia. The 70,800-square-foot store, which had formerly been an Upton's, provided five distinct furniture galleries for customers to shop from, as well as an Interactive Media Center that customers could use to create virtual renditions of rooms with furniture products for sale in the store.

Four months later, in November, Rich's opened its twenty-third department store, a two-story, 227,300-square-foot facility at the Mall of Georgia in Buford, Georgia, approximately thirty miles north of Atlanta off Interstate 85. Rich's had not originally planned to put a store at this mall when it opened in August 1999; however, the company reversed course when it discovered that Nordstrom planned to open a store there.

Less than a year after Rich's opened its Mall of Georgia store, the world witnessed the destruction of the South and North Towers of the World Trade Center in New York City by al Qaeda–affiliated plane hijackers on September 11, 2001. Executives at Rich's, as well as executives of other businesses across the country, grappled with not only their own personal feelings about the events but also the collective feelings of their companies and how they could express those feelings through an appropriate reaction to the devastation and loss of life that occurred that day. Almost immediately after the attacks, Federated made a donation to the American Red Cross and matched employee contributions, some of which came from Rich's, to the organization dollar-for-dollar up to a specified amount.

On the anniversary of 9/11 a year later, Rich's, along with Macy's, ran advertisements honoring those who had died, as well as the tragedy's heroes. Accompanying the Rich's ads were clip-out pledge cards for blood donations, billed as an ongoing need for many lifesaving organizations.

Sandwiched between 9/11 and its one-year anniversary was the opening of Rich's twenty-fourth suburban department store at The Mall at Stonecrest in Lithonia, Georgia, an eastern suburb of Atlanta. The store, which opened on October 18, 2001, two days before the rest of the mall opened and just over a month after 9/11, was composed of two floors equaling 160,000 square feet of retailing space.

Seven months later, in May 2002, Rich's opened its twenty-fifth suburban department store in Columbus, Georgia, a little over one hundred miles southwest of Atlanta. Like the citizens of Savannah who used to hop on the Nancy Hanks train to Atlanta for a day of shopping at Rich's, so had Columbus citizens hopped on the Man O' War streamliner that ran to Atlanta to do the same. Once the train ceased to run, trips by car ensued. Now, however, the city had its own Rich's, a one-story, 110,000-square-foot store, which opened in the former Montgomery Ward's space at the city's Peachtree Mall, immediately south of the city's airport off Interstate 185. Ironically, for as long as the city had waited for Rich's to come to town, it would only see the singular "Rich's" nameplate above the store for nine months before a new name replaced it, earning this store the distinction of being the last Rich's to open.

After opening the store in Columbus, Rich's parent, Federated, announced in August 2002 changes to store layouts and services to be tested at Rich's Town Center at Cobb, Lenox Square and North Point Mall stores in the Atlanta area by the end of the year. Some of these changes included introducing shopping carts, centralized checkouts, coed dressing rooms in junior departments, price tag scanners in certain areas of the store to verify

An interior view of the entrance to Rich's at Lenox Square mall, now a Macy's, circa early 2000s. *Courtesy of Stevens & Wilkinson, Inc.*

prices, refreshment areas and sit-down Internet stations. Also to be added at certain stores were free in-store child-care centers, named Playaways, much like Rich's had offered at its downtown Atlanta and Lenox Store locations in previous decades. However, once the new services were implemented, many customers disliked them and thought they were too similar to what discount retailers like Target and Walmart offered. As a result, many of them were done away with. These changes, however, were nothing compared to the change that was about to be implemented at Rich's, which would forever alter the history of the company.

Though many people had anticipated the move by Federated, loyal Rich's customers had hoped that what was announced by Federated on January 16, 2003, would never happen—the merging of Rich's with Macy's. For the previous eight years, both stores had operated in the same market within the same malls to attract the same customers. Many of these customers were new residents to Atlanta and other areas where Rich's operated and were not familiar or loyal to the chain, as older customers were. In addition, these customers thought the two stores were essentially the same, only operating with two different names.

From a business perspective, it was inevitable for the two stores to be merged. Federated wanted to strengthen its brand and eliminate the problems associated with "competing" stores in a crowded retail field. Additionally, the company wanted to streamline its operations in order to more effectively compete with discount retailers, such as Target and Walmart, which over the past several decades had slowly siphoned away traditional department store shoppers.

On February 2, 2003, it was official; Rich's and Macy's were merged, creating Rich's-Macy's. With the merger came changes to both previously separate store chains. In Atlanta, Macy's Southlake Mall, Gwinnett Place mall, Cumberland Mall and downtown Atlanta locations were closed. The Macy's store at Town Center at Cobb was closed and reopened as a Rich's-Macy's Furniture Gallery. The Macy's stores at Lenox Square and Perimeter Mall were closed and reopened as Bloomingdale's, allowing Federated to bring that chain to Atlanta. Other Macy's throughout the South were closed. The Macy's at Northlake Mall in northeastern Atlanta was closed and reopened as the first cobranded Rich's-Macy's, making it the twenty-sixth suburban department store to have Rich's name above its door, albeit sharing space with Macy's name. All of Rich's other stores throughout the South were converted to Rich's-Macy's stores.

Six months later, in August, Federated touted the Rich's-Macy's branding as a success and indicated that improved sales at these stores helped the company to decide to speed up plans to merge and cobrand other department stores under its control, such as Bon Marche, Burdines, Lazarus and Goldsmith's to Bon Marche–Macy's, Burdines-Macy's, Lazarus-Macy's and Goldsmith's-Macy's. In doing this, Federated could expand Macy's into new markets while keeping loyal customers of local chains. Many people believed, however, that it was only a matter of time before the local store names would be dropped altogether, leaving just Macy's on store marquees across the country. Further proof to these beliefs were the major ad campaigns that Federated was conducting at this time, which were heavily promoting the Macy's connection throughout the company's Macy's East, Macy's West and Rich's-Macy's divisions.

In keeping with its plans to streamline operations under recently cobranded stores, Federated announced in January 2004 that it was closing five underperforming stores. Two of those were Rich's-Macy's stores. In the Atlanta market, the Rich's-Macy's at Cobb Center in Smyrna, Georgia, was closed. Its popular furniture clearance section located on its second floor was moved to the Rich's-Macy's Furniture Gallery at Town Center at Cobb in neighboring Kennesaw, Georgia. In the Birmingham market, the Rich's-Macy's at Century Plaza in Irondale, Alabama, was closed. The other three of the five underperforming stores closed were Lazarus-Macy's stores in the Midwest.

Eight months later, Federated opened a Rich's-Macy's store on September 1, 2004, at Arbor Place Mall off Interstate 20 in Douglasville, Georgia, west of Atlanta. This two-story, 140,000-square-foot store, decorated with historic black-and-white photographs of Rich's Lenox Square mall and Greenbriar Mall stores, was the only store to be built from the ground up and open under the Rich's-Macy's moniker. It, the twenty-seventh suburban department store to have Rich's name on it, would also be the last store associated with the venerable retailer. Twelve days after it opened, Federated announced that it was dropping Rich's from its Rich's-Macy's department store names.

On September 13, 2004, Atlantans and those loyal to Rich's around the South (Richites) learned that their beloved retailing institution would soon no longer exist. Federated's plan to drop the Rich's name from its cobranded Rich's-Macy's stores was done in part to focus its efforts on its two core brands, Macy's and Bloomingdale's. Federated, too, knew that Macy's had established national appeal, if not international appeal, as a brand over the years because of its televised Thanksgiving Day parade and its portrayal in the 1947 perennial Christmas film classic *Miracle on 34th Street*, which trumped loyalty to a regional chain located in cities made up of many recent transplants, as was the case in Atlanta. Also added into this mix was that department stores were no longer the service-oriented, Disney-esque temples of retailing that they had once been, which had garnered them legions of loyal shoppers awed by their marketing savvy. People were now more loyal to their money and how far it would stretch instead of the hallowed name of the institution in which it was being spent.

Though no consolation to those who would be mourning the loss of Rich's from store nameplates in three states, Federated was actually removing other regional names from stores across the country. Within the next few months, Burdines from Burdines-Macy's, Bon Marche from Bon Marche–Macy's, Goldsmith's from Goldsmith's-Macy's and Lazarus from Lazarus-Macy's would join Rich's in the pile of discarded department store names once synonymous with the regions they served.

In January 2005, three and a half months after it announced plans to remove Rich's names from its stores, Federated commenced the physical process of doing so and gradually replaced Rich's-Macy's signage on stores throughout the South with new Macy's signage. Along with these external changes came internal changes, which involved stores swapping out Rich's-Macy's shopping bags and in-store signs for ones only displaying Macy's name. Customers, too, were receiving their new, replacement Macy's credit cards.

By March 6, Rich's was history; the day before had been the last day of its existence. The store that Morris Rich had started in the aftermath of the American Civil War in Atlanta was less than three months shy of celebrating its 138th birthday. The store that had blossomed into a southern institution was no more.

APPENDICES

RICH'S NOMENCLATURE

M. Rich & Co. (1867–1877)—May 28, 1867, store opened by Morris Rich

M. Rich & Bro. (1877–1884)—February 1, 1877, Emanuel Rich admitted to partnership

M. Rich & Bros. (1884–1901)—July 1, 1884, Daniel Rich admitted to partnership

M. Rich & Bros. Co. (1901–1929)—Petition for charter of incorporation filed December 20, 1900; charter granted January 12, 1901

Rich's, Inc. (1929–2003)—Per board of director's minutes of April 1, 1929, firm becomes Rich's, Inc. and M. Rich & Bros. Co. becomes a real estate company; this time period includes the October 29, 1976 Federated merger and the 1988 Rich's/Goldsmith's and 1995 Rich's/Lazarus/Goldsmith's Federated division mergers

Rich's-Macy's (2003–2005)— February 2, 2003, Federated merges Rich's and Macy's nameplates into one

Macy's (2005–present)—March 6, 2005, Federated drops Rich's name from Rich's-Macy's nameplate

LIST OF RICH'S STORES (1924–2004)

Downtown Atlanta (1924, closed 1991)
Rich's Military Store (circa 1943)
Out-of-Town Service Office (1948)
Knoxville (1955, closed 1961)
Belvedere Appliance Store (1956, closed 1959)
Lenox Square (1959)
Belvedere Plaza (1959, closed 1986)
Cobb Center (1963, closed 2004)
North DeKalb Mall (1965)
Greenbriar Mall (1965)
South DeKalb Mall (1969)
Discount Home Store (1971)
Perimeter Mall (1971)
Cumberland Mall (1973)
Brookwood Village (1974)
Century Plaza (1975, closed 2004)
Southlake Mall (1976)
Columbia Mall (1978)
Augusta Mall (1978)
Haywood Mall (1980)
Shannon Mall (1980)
Gwinnett Place (1984)
Riverchase Galleria (1986)
Town Center at Cobb (1986)
Rich's Furniture Showroom, Perimeter Mall (1986)
Oglethorpe Mall (1992)
North Point Mall (1993)
Rich's Furniture Showroom, Gwinnett Place (1998)
Macon Mall (1998)—formerly Macy's
Georgia Square Mall (1998)—formerly Macy's
Rich's North Point Furniture Showroom (2000)
Mall of Georgia (2000)
The Mall at Stonecrest (2001)
Peachtree Mall (2002)—formerly Montgomery Ward
Northlake Mall (2003)— formerly Macy's, opened as the first cobranded
    Rich's-Macy's
Arbor Place Mall (2004)—opened as Rich's-Macy's

RICH'S PRESIDENTS AND CHAIRMEN

Presidents

1901—Morris Rich
1926—Walter H. Rich
1947—Frank H. Neely
1949—Richard H. Rich
1961—Harold Brockey
1972—Joel Goldberg
1978—Allen I. Questrom
1980—James M. Zimmerman
1984—Merwin F. Kaminstein
1987—Roger N. Farah
1988—Winfrey Smith
1990—Carl Tooker
1991—Russell Stravitz
1993—Susan D. Kronick
1997—Arnold Orlick
1999—Edwin J. Holman
2000—David L. Nichols
2004—Michael Krauter

Chairmen

1926—Morris Rich
1949—Frank H. Neely
1961—Richard H. Rich
1972—Harold Brockey
1978—Joel Goldberg
1980—Allen I. Questrom
1984—James M. Zimmerman
1988—Roger N. Farah
1991—Carl Tooker
1993—Russell Stravitz
1999—Arnold Orlick
2001—Ronald Klein
2004—David L. Nichols
2005—Edwin J. Holman

NOTES

INTRODUCTION

1. Baker, *Rich's of Atlanta*, 6.

CHAPTER 1

2. Hanleiter, *Hanleiter's Atlanta City Directory*, for 1870, 5.
3. *Atlanta Constitution*, December 10, 1872, 3; February 22, 1874, 8; March 8, 1874, 8.

CHAPTER 2

4. Ibid., December 31, 1876, 4.
5. Sibley, *Dear Store*, 95.
6. *Atlanta Constitution*, May 18, 1879, 4.

CHAPTER 3

7. Authors Henry Givens Baker and Celestine Sibley in their books on Rich's improperly state that Haverty was hired as manager after Emanuel Rich's

suicide in 1897. Baker based his account of Haverty on a May 1937 story in *Rich Bits* written by Elton Sauls, "The Gay Nineties." He did no other research to confirm facts. Sibley copied Baker's story. In July 1894, J.J. Haverty and A.G. Rhodes had gone into business with P.H. Snook, forming the Rhodes, Snook & Haverty Furniture Company. In January 1897, this furniture business dissolved, and Rhodes-Haverty's was reformed and remained in business until 1908, when they parted ways and Haverty was on his own. In July 1897, Emanuel Rich committed suicide. There is no historical evidence to support the claim that Haverty went back to work at Rich's. No newspaper articles exist in the summer and fall of 1897 showing Haverty at Rich's. There are, however, ads placed at this time looking for men to work in Rich's furniture department.

8. *Atlanta Constitution*, January 4, 1885, 9; July 11, 1886, 15; August 1, 1886, 10.

9. Ibid., October 21, 1888, 18; April 21, 1889, 21.

Chapter 4

10. Ibid., April 28, 1907, A8.

11. *Atlanta Journal*, May 31, 1910, 10–11.

12. The basement actually moved to the Store for Homes on July 7, 1947, months before the rest of the building was ready to be occupied. In 1967, the author's own mother bought her wedding dress from the store.

Chapter 5

13. *Atlanta Constitution*, March 23, 1924, 1, 7–8; Baker, *Rich's of Atlanta*, 170.

14. Baker, *Rich's of Atlanta*, 178.

15. Mrs. Harrington's, née Amelie Adams, husband was William Eugene Harington, a founding member and partner of Spratlin, Harrington & Thomas, an insurance and real estate mortgage business.

16. Over subsequent years, the model of a department store having a personal shopping bureau under the guise of a single female name became quite common. Miami's Burdines department store's similar service was titled "Jane Gray," and Allentown, Pennsylvania's Hess's department store's service was titled "Sarah Moffett."

17. *Atlanta Constitution*, January 28, 1925, 13.

Chapter 7

18. Edwards, *Road to Tara*, 211.

19. Within a few years of being rechristened the Magnolia Room, America's "second Audubon," painter Athos Menaboni, who was born in Italy but was a resident of Atlanta, sketched/painted a series of five works (deer, seagulls, a brown thrasher in blackberries, cardinals in magnolias and a butterfly in cotton blossoms) that were used on the Magnolia Room's menu covers. In February 1948, the works were displayed in the Georgia Exhibit at the Library of Congress in Washington, D.C.

20. *Atlanta Constitution*, January 28, 1942, 14.

21. *Rich Bits*, September 1967, Third Centennial Issue, 12.

22. The "W" call letter indicated that the station was east of the Mississippi; "ABE" stands for Atlanta Board of Education.

23. On November 3, 1974, while walking home from a friend's house in St. Augustine, Florida, where she had retired, Bemis was bludgeoned to death with a cement block. Some speculate her murder was in retribution for a tell-all book she was planning to write on the murder of her friend and neighbor, former model and socialite Athalia Ponsell Lindsley, which had occurred ten months prior to Bemis's murder. To this day, both cases remain unsolved.

24. Sibley, *Dear Store*, 135.

25. *Atlanta Journal-Constitution*, "Peach Buzz: Animal Fund Protest Stirs Fur Fury at Fox," September 10, 1989, A/2.

26. Telephone interview with Shelia Kamensky Gerstein, April 8, 2011, and follow-up e-mails, April 17 and May 31, 2011.

27. "Letting customers make their own adjustments"—per Frank Neely's 1951 advertising policies found in Baker, *Rich's of Atlanta*, 294: "The implication of this announcement was carried out by definite instructions to everyone in Rich's employ to refrain from stating other position than that assumed by the customer. The customer was only to be asked the simple question: 'What do you want us to do about it?'" in regards to making allowances or adjustments on any unsatisfactory purchase or transactions that had been made.

28. Sibley, *Dear Store*, 138.

29. For the first three or four years of the tree-lighting event, choirs performed on only one side of the bridge. By the early 1950s, however, choirs had been installed on each side so that no matter what side of the bridge someone was looking at they could see the choral performances.

30. The year 1957 was a guess. The windows were not there in 1956 and were by 1959. In newspaper ads, it appears that they were there in 1958, but the ads were blurred and hard to make out.

31. *Atlanta Journal-Constitution*, "Great Tree Had Stand-In: Event Manager Uses Quick Recovery to Tout Its Expertise," November 25, 2004, JF24.

32. Different stories exist as to whether it was Walter Rich or Morris Rich who asked Dick to change his last name to Rich. The story as told by Henry Givens Baker and Celestine Sibley, which Dick would have known about, was that it was Walter. Some family members insist it was Morris.

Chapter 8

33. *Atlanta Constitution*, July 10, 1950, 13.

34. News cameras from WROL-TV (now WATE-TV) captured the events on film, which is available in certain archives for viewing; in the author's files donated to the Atlanta History Center is a copy of this film.

35. Named Endowment Funds, www.lovett.org.

36. E-mail interview with Kim Blass, May 31, 2011.

37. Telephone interview with Gerstein, April 8, 2011, and follow-up e-mails, April 17 and May 31, 2011.

38. Despite the fact that Rich's has officially stated for more than three decades that the Pink Pig first appeared at its downtown Atlanta store in 1953, that date is incorrect, nor was the ride first known as the Pink Pig. It is not known for certain why that year has been widely assumed as the year the Pink Pig made its first appearance at Rich's. The date, however, has been repeatedly used, as evidenced in a press release distributed by the company in 1991 when the downtown Rich's store was closed and the Pink Pig, subsequently, had to find a new home ("The Pink Pig Rides Again," Rich's press release, August 8, 1991). Telephone interview with Jay Salzman, February 9, 2011, and follow-up e-mail, April 25, 2011.

39. Dr. William L. Bird Jr. e-mail to the author, February 24, 2011. Bird is the curator of the Division of Political History at the Smithsonian Institution and the author of *Holidays on Display*. Bird's e-mail contained his original research notes on the Rocket Express Systems monorails, which contained information culled from 1948 and 1949 issues of *Display World*.

40. Ibid.

41. *Atlanta Constitution*, October 12, 1956, 23.

42. *Atlanta Journal-Constitution*, Rich's ad, October 28, 1956, 11-B.

43. *Business Week*, "The Stores Say It With Lights," December 14, 1957.

44. Telephone interview with Salzman, February 9, 2011, and follow-up e-mail, April 25, 2011.

45. *Atlanta Journal-Constitution*, Rich's ad, December 6, 1959, 16-B.

46. Melissa Goff e-mail to the author, March 29, 2011. Goff is vice-president of media relations and cause marketing at Macy's.

47. The square footage for this suburban store and all others are approximations. Sources often varied, contradicting one another.

CHAPTER 9

48. *Atlanta Journal*, "Rich's Tells 7 Negroes About Separate Grills," March 8, 1960, 3.

49. Lonnie King was followed in command by Atlanta University student co-chair John Mack, who, after graduating in the spring of 1960, was succeeded by Spelman College student Herschelle Sullivan in September 1960.

50. Details uncovered by Jack Bass in his book, *Taming the Storm*. Bass's editor, Jacqueline Kennedy Onassis, confirmed his account of JFK and MLK during those months of October 1960, telling him he "was a very good investigative reporter" (from an e-mail from Jack Bass to the author, April 12, 2011).

51. Despite Rich's integration, the company found itself under attack over subsequent years for discriminatory practices. On November 21, 1963, 400 students (from the AU Center, GA Tech and Emory) picketed in front of Rich's downtown Atlanta store during rush hour, demanding that the company hire more black personnel and upgrade those black workers already at the company to something other than menial jobs. The protest was led by Reverend Ralph Abernathy, at the time secretary treasurer of the Southern Christian Leadership Conference, and Larry Fox, head of the Atlanta University Committee on Appeal for Human Rights. On April 3, 1973, 350 employees walked out of Rich's claiming discrimination in hiring, pay and promotion practices. Led by Hosea Williams, a prominent civil rights participant, the strike ensued for seven weeks but ultimately ended when the strikers accepted mediation by the Community Relations Commission. On a positive note, the company hired its first black member to its board of directors, Jesse Hill, in the early 1970s. Hill was chief executive of Atlanta Life, the largest privately held black business in the nation, and was also co-founder of the *Atlanta Inquirer*, a progressive black newspaper. In August 1980, Rich's opened

its Shannon Mall store, employing Gail Nutt as the company's first black store manager.

52. "The true church" of the South, Sibley, *Dear Store*, 12; "Warner Sallman's Head of Christ" is inaccurately referred to by Sibley as "Salzman's 'Head of Christ,'" *Dear Store*, 106.

53. Ibid., 254.

54. A reference to Tom Mahoney's article, "The Store That Married a City," which appeared in the *Saturday Evening Post*, December 3, 1949, 34, 176–78.

55. Telephone interview with Jim Seigler, February 21, 2011.

Chapter 10

56. There may have been more Rich's IIs than recorded here; however, attempts to ascertain the accurate number of stores came to no avail. Former Rich's employees and current Macy's officials had no easily accessible records of the boutique to confirm numbers. Other sources, such as the *Atlanta Journal-Constitution* and Rich's *Rich Bits* or annual reports, offered scant information on the boutiques.

57. Per Dupree, her restaurant had multiple names over the years—Mt. Pleasant Village, Nathalie's Mt. Pleasant Village, etc.

58. Telephone interview with Nathalie Dupree, March 21, 2011, and multiple follow-up e-mails from then to June 2011.

Chapter 11

59. *Federated Department Stores, Inc. 1976 Annual Report*, 17.

Chapter 12

60. E-mail interview with Neil Shorthouse, April 16, 2011.

61. The ABC *World News Tonight* program aired January 3, 1990; Iacoca's visit was on March 22, 1990, and he did end up opening a CIS center at Lehigh, titled the National Center for Partnership Development.

62. Brack, *Gwinnett*, 581–82.

63. Telephone interview with Robert Reiser, June 8, 2011.

64. "Employee Volunteerism Programs," www.macysinc.com, as of June 2011.

BIBLIOGRAPHY

INTERVIEWS

Asher, Thomas. Personal interview, November 16, 2010.
———. Personal interview, December 23, 2010.
Berg, Anne. Personal interview, October 22, 2010.
———. Personal interview, November 16, 2010.
Blass, Kim. E-mail interview, May 31, 2011.
Dendy, Carl. Personal interview, April 10, 2011.
Dupree, Nathalie. Telephone interview, March 21, 2011.
Gerstein, Shelia Kamensky. Telephone interview, April 8, 2011.
———. Telephone interview, April 17, 2011.
King, Lonnie C. Personal interview, June 16, 2011.
Orbert-Nelson, Blondean. Telephone interview, October 18, 2011.
Pflum, Patricia. E-mail interview, April 16, 2011.
Salzman, Jay. Telephone interview, February 9, 2011.
Seigler, Jim. Telephone interview, February 21, 2011.
Shorthouse, Neil. E-mail interview, April 17, 2011.

PERIODICALS

Atlanta Constitution
Atlanta Journal
Atlanta Journal-Constitution

Atlanta Magazine
Business Week
Cincinnati Enquirer
Columbus Ledger-Enquirer
Crain's
Display World
Esquire
Federated Department Stores, Inc. Annual Reports
Federated Department Stores, Inc. Corporate Fact Book
Federated's Coast to Coast
Federated's focal point
Federated's In Focus
Forbes
Fortune
Glamour
Greenville News
Knoxville News-Sentinel
Manhattan, inc.
New York Times
Rich Bits
Richbits
Rich's and You
Rich's, Inc. Annual Reports
Rich's Little Bits
Rich's news bits
Rich's: People
Saturday Evening Post
Stores
Time
Wall Street Journal
Women's Wear Daily

OTHER SOURCES

Asher, Norman. "Various Subjects: History of Rich's, Including His Role and His Father's Role at the Store." E-mails to author, 2011–12.

Asher, Thomas. "Various Subjects: Rich's History, The Rich Foundation, Leadership, Stores, et al." E-mails to author, 2010–12.

Auchmutey, Jim. "Pink Pig." E-mail to author, October 2010.

Baker, Henry Givens. *Rich's of Atlanta: The Story of a Store Since 1867*. Atlanta, GA: Foote & Davies, 1953.

Barnwell, V.T. *Barnwell's Atlanta City Directory, and Strangers' Guide: Also, a General Firemen's, Church, Masonic, and Odd-Fellows' Record*. Vol. 1. Atlanta, GA: Intelligencer Book and Job Office, 1867.

Bass, Jack. *Taming the Storm: The Life and Times of Judge Frank M. Johnson, Jr., and the South's Fight over Civil Rights*. New York: Doubleday, 1993.

———. "Various Subjects: MLK Sit-in at Rich's and JFK." E-mails to author, 2011–12.

Berg, Anne. "Various Subjects: Discussion about Various Aspects of Rich's, Particularly in Regards to Celestine Sibley and Her Book." E-mails to author, 2010–12.

Bird, William L., Jr. *Holidays on Display*. New York: Princeton Architectural Press, 2007.

Blass, Kim. "Lovett Fashion Shows." E-mails to author, 2011.

Blumberg, Janice Rothschild. *One Voice: Rabbi Jacob M. Rothschild and the Troubled South*. Macon, GA: Mercer University Press, 1985.

Brack, Elliott E. *Gwinnett: A Little above Atlanta: A Modern History of Gwinnett County*. Norcross, GA: Brack Group Inc. (dba GwinnettForum) and United Writers Press, Inc., 2008.

Branch, Taylor. *Parting the Waters: America in the King Years 1954–63*. New York: Simon & Schuster Inc., 1989.

Campbell, Donald. "Stevens & Wilkinson." E-mails to author, 2011–12.

Clarke, E.Y. *Illustrated History of Atlanta*. Atlanta, GA: Jas. P. Harrison & Co., 1877.

Clemmons, Archie. Square footage calculations. Telephone calls, 2011–12.

Clemmons, Greg. "Civil Rights." E-mails to author, 2011–12.

Dendy, Carl. "Rich's Bake Shops." E-mails to author, 2010–11.

Dupree, Nathalie. "Rich's Cooking School." E-mails to author, 2010–11.

EDAW, Inc. "Rich's Downtown Department Store (Rich's Downtown)." Historic Buildings Survey Report (HABS No. GA-2290). Washington, D.C.: U.S. Department of the Interior, National Park Service, 1994.

Edwards, Anne. *Road to Tara: The Life of Margaret Mitchell*. New Haven, CT: Ticknor & Fields, 1983.

Elvins, Sarah. "Scrip, Stores, and Cash-Strapped Cities: American Retailers and Alternative Currency during the Great Depression." *Journal of Historical Research in Marketing* 2, no. 1 (2010): 86–107.

Fleming, Cynthia Griggs. "White Lunch Counters and Black Consciousness: The Story of the Knoxville Sit-ins." *Tennessee Historical Quarterly* 49, no. 1 (1990): 40–52.

Fruchtman, Ellen. "Penelope Penn." E-mails to author, 2011.

Gardner, Mark L. "Rich's of Atlanta—Does a Change of Ownership Affect Corporate Culture." *Essays in Economic and Business History* 2 (1993): 272–82.

Garrett, Franklin M. *Atlanta and Environs: A Chronicle of Its People and Events.* New York: Lewis Historical Publishing Company, Inc., 1954.

Gerstein, Shelia Kamensky. "Fashionata and Lovett Fashion Shows." E-mails to author, 2011.

Goff, Melissa. "Various Subjects: History of Rich's, Pink Pigs, Macy's, Significant Dates and Photo Usage." E-mails to author, 2011–12.

Grady-Willis, Winston A. *Challenging U.S. Apartheid: Atlanta and Black Struggles for Human Rights, 1960–1977.* Durham, NC: Duke University Press, 2006.

Greene, Melissa Fay. *The Temple Bombing.* Reading, MA: Addison-Wesley Publishing Company, 1996.

Hanleiter, William R. *Hanleiter's Atlanta City Directory, for 1870.* The First Annual Issue. Atlanta, GA: William R. Hanleiter, Publisher, 1870.

Harris, Leon. *Merchant Princes: An Intimate History of Jewish Families Who Built Great Department Stores.* New York: Harper & Row, 1979.

Haverty, Rawson. *Ain't the Roses Sweet.* Atlanta, GA: private printing, 1989.

Historic Preservation Consulting. "Historic Resources Report: A Part of the Cultural Resource Assessment for the Proposed Federal Center Atlanta, Georgia." Avondale Estates, GA: Historic Preservation Consulting, 1993.

Hunt, William G. "College of Arms." E-mails to author, 2011–12.

Jones, Sharon Foster. "Various Subjects: Morris, Maud, Emanuel Rich Photographs for Use in Book, as Well as General Information in Regards to Book and the Process of Writing It." E-mails to author, 2011–12.

King, Lonnie C. "MLK Sit-in at Rich's, 1960." E-mails to author, 2011–12.

Klein, Sharron. "Various Subjects: Mrs. Harrington and Atlanta Junior League's Roles at Rich's Over the Years." E-mails to author, 2011–12.

Knight, Gladys. *Between Each Line of Pain and Glory: My Life Story.* New York: Hyperion, 1997.

Kruse, Kevin M. *White Flight: Atlanta and the Making of Modern Conservatism.* Princeton, NJ: Princeton University Press, 2005.

Kuhn, Clifford M., Harlon E. Joye and E. Bernard West. *Living Atlanta: An Oral History of the City, 1914–1948.* Athens: University of Georgia Press, 2005.

Lefever, Harry G. *Undaunted by the Fight: Spelman College and the Civil Rights Movement, 1957–1967.* Macon, GA: Mercer University Press, 2005.

Mahoney, Tom. "The Store That Married a City." *Saturday Evening Post,* December 3, 1949: 34, 176–78.

Merritt, Carole. "Interview with Lonnie King." Atlanta History Center, November 21, 2005.

Minatra, Dixie. "Rich's History." E-mails to author, 2011.

Mitchell, William R., Jr. *J. Neel Reid Architect of Hentz, Reid & Adler and the Georgia School of Classicists.* Savannah, GA: Golden Coast Publishing Company, 1997.

Montag, Anthony. "Rich's Book." E-mails to author, March 2012.

New Georgia Encyclopedia. www.georgiaencyclopedia.org.

The New Georgia Guide. Athens: University of Georgia Press, 1996.

Orbert-Nelson, Blondean. "Sit-ins of 1960." E-mails to author, 2012.

Pflum, Patricia. "Rich's Academy." E-mails to author, April 2011.

Pioneer Citizens' Society of Atlanta. *History of Atlanta and Its Pioneers.* Atlanta, GA: Byrd Printing Company, 1902.

Pomerantz, Gary M. *Where Peachtree Meets Sweet Auburn: A Saga of Race and Family.* New York: Penguin Books, 1997.

Pope, Roslyn, et al. *An Appeal for Human Rights.* March 1960.

Proudfoot, Merrill. *Diary of a Sit-In.* Chapel Hill: University of North Carolina Press, 1962.

Raines, Howell. *My Soul Is Rested: Movement Days in the Deep South Remembered.* New York: Penguin Books, 1987.

Ramsey, Tom. "Stevens & Wilkinson." E-mails to author, 2011–12.

Reed, Wallace P., ed. *History of Atlanta, Georgia.* Syracuse, NY: D. Mason & Co., 1889.

Reiser, Robert. "Carol Dunlap Reiser—Partners in Time." E-mail to R. Reiser, May 20, 2011, followed by telephone call from R. Reiser to author.

Richard H. Rich papers (1902–1981), Manuscript Collection No. 575, Manuscript, Archives and Rare Book Library, Emory University.

Rich's Department Store, MSS 708, Kenan Research Center, Atlanta History Center.

Rich's-Macy's. *I Rode the Pink Pig: Atlanta's Favorite Christmas Tradition.* Athens, GA: Hill Street Press, 2004.

Russell, James Michael. *Atlanta 1847–1890: City Building in the Old South and the New.* Baton Rouge: Louisiana State University Press, 1988.

Schairer, Joan. "Genealogy of the Riches and Mrs. Harrington and Mrs. Lott Warren Jr." E-mails to author, 2010–12.

Schairer, Lois. "Rich's: Discussions on Rich Family Tree, Mrs. Harrington, Mrs. Lott Warren Jr. and Ship Logs." E-mails to author, 2010–12.

Seigler, Jim, and Ellen Seigler. "Atlanta from the Ashes." E-mails to author, 2011–12.

Shorthouse, Neil. "Rich's Academy." E-mails to author, April 2011.

Sibley, Celestine. *Dear Store: An Affectionate Portrait of Rich's.* Garden City, NY: Doubleday & Company, 1967.

Sluzewski, Jim. "Various Subjects: History of Rich's, Store Information, Name and Positions at Rich's, Federated, Macy's and Significant Dates." E-mails to author, 2011–12.

Smith, William Rawson. *Villa Clare: The Purposeful Life and Timeless Art Collection of J.J. Haverty.* Macon, GA: Mercer University Press, 2006.

Snider, Rick, ed. *The Road Atlanta Yearbook 1978.* Atlanta, GA: private printing, 1978.

Stevens, Preston Standish. *Building a Firm: The Story of Stevens & Wilkinson Architects Engineers Planners Inc.* Atlanta, GA: Williams Printing Co., 1979.

Stevens, Preston, Jr. "Stevens & Wilkinson." E-mails to author, 2011–12.

Taylor, Barbara Cable. *The Life and Art of Athos Menaboni.* Macon, GA: Mercer University Press, 2000.

Vanek, Elizabeth. Telephone call, November 5, 2011.

Washington, James M., ed. *A Testament of Hope: The Essential Writings and Speeches of Martin Luther King, Jr.* New York: HarperCollins, 1991.

Waugh-Benton, Monica. "Strike Fever: Labor Unrest, Civil Rights and the Left in Atlanta, 1972." (2006). *History Theses.* Paper 16. digitalarchive.gsu.edu/history_theses/16.

Weitnauer, John. "Richway." E-mails to author, 2012.

Whitaker, Jan. *Service and Style: How the American Department Store Fashioned the Middle Class.* New York: St. Martin's Press, 2006.

ABOUT THE AUTHOR

Although born in Alabama, Jeff Clemmons considers himself an Atlantan, having lived in the metropolitan area for the past twenty-six years. His family has an even older connection to the city, with his great-great-grandfather Archibald Clemmons fighting in the Atlanta Campaign, including the Battle of Atlanta, during the American Civil War.

Clemmons has a degree in business administration from Reinhardt University and a degree in creative writing from Georgia State University. His current full-time employer is an international law firm based in Atlanta, where he works in the public relations department.

Courtesy of Greg Clemmons.

Outside of his day-to-day job, he gives walking tours that he created of the Midtown and SoNo districts of Atlanta for the Atlanta Preservation Center. He also serves on the board of the Atlanta Preservation Center's auxiliary group, CIRCA, which offers its members private tours of some of metropolitan Atlanta's most interesting historical structures.

All of Clemmons's research for *Rich's: A Southern Institution* is housed at the Atlanta History Center.

Visit us at
www.historypress.net